# THE TRAGEDY TEST

# THE TRAGEDY TEST

*Making Sense of Life-Changing Loss*
*—A Rabbi's Journey—*

RICHARD AGLER

RESOURCE *Publications* · Eugene, Oregon

THE TRAGEDY TEST
Making Sense of Life-Changing Loss—A Rabbi's Journey

Resource Publications
An Imprint of Wipf and Stock Publishers
199 W. 8th Ave., Suite 3
Eugene, OR 97401

www.wipfandstock.com

PAPERBACK ISBN: 978-1-5326-5792-4
HARDCOVER ISBN: 978-1-5326-5793-1
EBOOK ISBN: 978-1-5326-5794-8

Manufactured in the U.S.A.                                    10/03/18

Grateful acknowledgment is made to the following for permission to reprint previously published material:

The Jewish Publication Society for "TANAKH: The Holy Scriptures: The New JPS Translation According to the Traditional Hebrew Text." Philadelphia: 1988. (Some translations have been modified by the author.)

The excerpt from the poem "Two Worlds Exist" is reprinted from Two Worlds Exist, copyright © 2016 by Yehoshua November, by permission of Orison Books, Inc. www.orisonbooks.com

A portion of the proceeds from the sale of this book will be donated to the Tali Fund, Inc.

For Talia

"We cannot live in the afternoon of life
according to the program of life's morning.
For what was great in the morning will be little use at evening
and what in the morning was true,
at evening will have become a lie."
—CARL JUNG

# Contents

# PART III—ACCEPTANCE

# Preface

WHY DID THIS HAPPEN? To me of all people? How could God let it? Why do good people suffer? Where is life's justice and fairness? How will I go on?

These are not new questions. Tragedy, especially when it hits us personally, has challenged our understanding of the Universe, and whatever God may be in it, for millennia.

This book is a personal response to a personal tragedy. When my twenty-six-year-old daughter was killed in an accident, it shook my life and it shook my faith. I did not know what would become of either one. I only knew that I would go forward with as much strength and courage as I could muster.

At the same time this book is rabbinic—unavoidably so. Having served some thirty-five years in the congregational rabbinate, it could hardly be otherwise. I am attempting to speak here as I would to a member of the community who is seeking understanding. I am also speaking to myself.

It has been said that that which is most personal is also most universal. I believe what is written here has meaning for intrepid questioners of every faith, for people with no active faith, and even for those who may doubt faith altogether. It offers a reasoned understanding of God that faithful and skeptic alike may find helpful—and perhaps even acceptable.

Tragedy tests our faith as nothing else does. And it is in the wake of tragedy that we most need it. Sooner or later, we all experience loss. Sooner or later, we, along with our faith and our God, whatever shape or form they may take, will face questions we cannot answer. Sooner or later, we all take the Tragedy Test.

I don't claim to have aced it. This is a record of how, by my own lights at least, I've managed to pass it.

I hope that this account of my journey will be of assistance to you on yours.

# Part I—CHALLENGE

# 1

# Talia Faith Agler, 1985–2012

"Nothing ever becomes real 'til it is experienced."[1]
—JOHN KEATS

AT ABOUT 11:40 P.M. on January 26, 2012, a Thursday night, the phone rang at our home in Florida. A strange voice asked for Mr. Agler, which let me know that it was not a rabbinic issue. Had it been, she would have asked for Rabbi Agler. I assumed it was some kind of scam, though the hour seemed late for that.

The caller identified herself as an officer of the United States Park Police and said she was calling from my daughter's apartment in Washington, DC. How bizarre, I thought. She asked once more, "Is this Mr. Agler?" I answered, "Yes."

Then it came. The officer told me that our daughter Talia had been in an accident, a serious one, and was in critical condition at George Washington University Hospital. She put Tali's apartment mate on the line, who confirmed everything in a familiar voice. This was no scam. It was the phone call that is every parent's worst nightmare.

They were able to patch through the Emergency Room doctor, who said I should get to the hospital as quickly as possible. I

1. Keats, *Letter,* 1819

3

explained that there were surely no flights from Florida to Washington until the next morning. The doctor said that would be all right. She also let me know—with consummate sensitivity and professionalism, making references to oxygen depletion, brain trauma, and the like—that, in as many words, the chances for Talia's survival were essentially nil.

I woke my wife Mindy with the news. As the police officer and doctor had done for me, I tried to break it to her as carefully as possible, but there was no sugarcoating the awful truth.

A series of midnight phone calls followed. The first was to our son Jesse and his wife Tovah, who lived nearby. They came right over. Next we called our daughter Sarah in New York. She would book an early flight and meet us in Washington. We called several of our cousins in the DC area to ask if they could go to the hospital to be with Tali. Every one of them said yes. Finally, we contacted the airline for seats on the morning's first flight.

When we arrived at the hospital, Tali was on a ventilator, surrounded by our cousins, several of her dear friends, and medical staff. Although she looked peaceful, it was clear to everyone that a tragedy of the first magnitude had taken place. She was pronounced dead that afternoon.

It was a shock on every level. Talia was a vibrant, healthy, and dynamic young woman. She was bright, fastidious, and careful to a fault. She worked in the field of international development for a large company, which had, earlier on the day of the accident and unbeknownst to her, approved her next promotion. After work, she went out for a jog along the National Mall and was struck by a motor vehicle. Mercifully, the doctors emphasized to us, she did not know what hit her.

There were two memorial services—one in Washington where she lived, worked and graduated from college, and another in Florida, where she grew up. Between them, over 1500 people attended. Love, hugs, and tributes came from family, friends, teachers, and associates near and far. Thousands of hits were recorded on the websites established in her memory. In the most horrific way possible, it was beautiful.

As her parents, we had much to be proud of and a great deal to be thankful for. Still, our grief was beyond words.

During my tenure as a congregational rabbi, it all too often fell to me to be with families in similar circumstances. Though I always gave it my best—and there were those who could not thank me enough—I never felt equal to the task. Now I understood why. No one—at least no one who has not gone through it themselves—has any idea what this is like.

## HER LIFE

Talia was born on April 9, 1985. She was the second of our three children, following her older brother Jesse by three years and preceding her younger sister Sarah by four.

She distinguished herself early on. Her first word was actually two, a question, "Where's Jess?" Right away we suspected that we had a hyper-verbal and inquisitive child on our hands, and in fact, we did. Tali was loquacious and charming, her company cherished by friends, teachers, extended family, and strangers alike. When she wasn't talking, she was reading—immersing herself in books of every description and loving the understanding and adventure she found there.

Coming of age in a rabbinic household, she absorbed the message that it is important to live for others, not only ourselves. She became passionate about social justice and was dedicated to making the world a better place.

When the opportunity to study for a semester abroad presented itself in college, she chose to do so in Nairobi, Kenya. She interned at a fledgling institution, the Centre for Domestic Training and Development, whose mission was to train impoverished East Africans to qualify for jobs as domestic workers.

This is a larger task than it may sound to Westerners. But for people who came from homes without electricity, running water or refrigeration—to say nothing of education—it was no small challenge. The CDTD became a success and has now graduated hundreds of students who have transformed their lives and climbed the socio-economic ladder.

Tali was proud to have taught there, and it left a strong impression on her. She sought work in the field of international development and was eventually hired by a major firm in Washington, who assigned her to their Africa desk. She kept in touch with the CDTD, and shortly before her death, its founder, Edith Murogo, discussed with her the possibility of establishing a rescue home for girls who were victims of trafficking and abuse. Tali enthusiastically endorsed the idea. After she died, Edith and her board named it in her honor: The Talia Agler Girls Shelter.

As an organ donor, Talia saved the lives of five people. In the process, she saved their families from the kind of loss we had just suffered. Her example inspired countless others to register and become donors themselves. Jewish tradition teaches that if you save one life, it is as if you have saved an entire world.[2] The number of lives that will be saved, and the family circles that will be sustained by her example, is incalculable.

A scholarship fund for college students at the Religious Action Center of Reform Judaism in Washington, DC was established in her name. In addition, our family launched a foundation, The Tali Fund, to continue her work. None of this would have happened had she not been the person she was.

As befit her middle name, Talia also had faith. She enjoyed studying religious texts, both ancient and modern. She believed that faith in general—and Judaism in particular—had much to contribute to the improvement of the world. One of her college professors, unaware of her background, suggested she become a rabbi. Tali thought that one in the family was enough.

Her personal ethic was one of giving. She was constantly phoning parents, grandparents, friends, and cousins, just to say hello.

There were also what we called "Tali-isms" or The Rules According to Tali:

- Always look shopkeepers, wait staff, and toll takers in the eye, and smile at them.

- Always ask questions—and keep asking until you understand the answer.

- Be a vegetarian but cook great meat dishes for your carnivore friends.

- Never sleep in your own bed if you have company visiting.

2. *Babylonian Talmud, Sanhedrin* 37a.

- Always pick up your friends at the airport—no cabs or trains for them.
- Family comes first—but everybody is family.
- Tell the people you love that you love them, every chance you get.

When people told me what a good job we had done as parents, I answered that I could accept partial credit, but Mindy gets more credit, and Tali gets full credit.

She was an extraordinary young woman—beautiful, intelligent, and winning. When her life came to an unexpected and premature end, it was traumatic for everyone who knew her.

When Tali died, the Tragedy Test hit us between the eyes. It said, "Let's see you deal with this; let's see you even try to pass it."

## THE AFTERMATH

"People by nature desire to know."[3]

—Aristotle

The questions came immediately: How could this happen? To someone so young? To someone so good? In a world purportedly overseen by a just and loving God?

On one level, when a two-ton vehicle strikes a one-hundred-pound person, it is clear what the outcome will be. The physics are no mystery. But what of the metaphysics? What kind of Higher Power, if any, allows such a thing to happen?

We've all heard people's responses to such situations: Good people are not supposed to die before their time. Parents should not have to bury their children. Time will heal. And so on. None of these brought us any comfort, let alone understanding.

We were not dealing with new questions. Sages and philosophers—both secular and religious—have wrestled with them since belief in a Just God first arose. As a rabbi, I was well acquainted with the dialectic. I had studied it in seminary, taught it in classes, and counseled it with families in need.

But the impact of Talia's death went beyond whatever academic or pastoral knowledge I possessed. The spiritual foundation I had built over the years kept me from going over the edge—but that edge was looming closer than comfort would have it.

Moreover, the issue needed to be addressed right away. It was going to be on the mind of everyone attending the services in her memory. People were asking: How could this happen? To her of all people? To such a good family? Even, To you, Rabbi? To leave these questions unaddressed was not an option.

At the memorials, I offered that faith was central to Mindy and me as we parented Tali and her siblings—each of them now outstanding adults in their own right. It was faith that enabled us to instill in her a measure of the purpose, character, and love that

3. Aristotle, *Metaphysics* I.1

came to define her life. Considering the person she became, how could we turn away from anything as precious as this?

Many people told us that these words had a powerful impact. My local Orthodox rabbinic colleague posted its essence online.[4] It was strong for me too, but it was incomplete. It may have addressed the importance of faith in building a good life, but it did nothing to help explain an untimely death.

§

My faith in the God who is just, kind, and true was longstanding. This was the God I prayed to, spoke about, and did my best to serve. I believed that people who were faithful to this God would receive blessing. When asked to account for life's inevitable injustices, I always acknowledged that there were things that did not add up. There would always be matters we did not understand and questions we could not answer. That was an honest response as far as it went. Now its shortcomings were greater than I could accept.

Clergy of every denomination are aware of the challenges that belief in a just God presents. The same is true for any person who has considered the subject seriously. The death of our daughter tested the faith I had lived, professed, taught, and attempted to exemplify, as nothing before.

My faith had shaped my life, for strength and blessing, in so many ways. I thought it would survive, though I wasn't sure how. I was going to let the process of wrestling with it take me wherever it led. I understood it was going to take time, and that it would mean leaving my comfort zone. But there was no other path.

I recalled the words of a friend who once said, "No one gets through life unscathed." His words left an impression because up until that point, my life had been, more or less, trauma-free. Sure, there were ups and downs, successes and failures—but nothing so devastating as to warrant the term *scathing*. With Talia's death, that came to an end. It was a shock to my emotions, my outlook, my

4. Goldberg, *Rabbi's Blog*, Feb. 10, 2012.

psyche, and my soul. I was not the same person. And my faith—my rabbinic faith no less—was not giving me what I needed. I have spent much of the time since Tali's death searching. I will doubtless spend more. There is still much that I do not understand and there is certainly much that I never will. I have rejected answers I once found acceptable and accepted answers I once rejected. My faith survived, but it is different than it was before. So is my understanding of the God I thought I knew.

## AT THE WESTERN WALL

"I knew that faith relied heavily on metaphors.
I did not know that so many of them would fail so spectacularly."[5]

In June of 2013, for the first time since Talia's death seventeen months earlier, I stood at the Western Wall in Jerusalem. It is known in Hebrew as the *Kotel Ha-Ma'aravi,* or *Kotel,* for short. It is considered Judaism's holiest site. I was there to pray.

The *Kotel* has long been a place of sacred encounter for me. I've been to Jerusalem many times over the years, and I make it my business to visit whenever I'm in the city. According to an old joke, "You can talk to God from anywhere, but in Jerusalem it's a local call." It seems even more local at the *Kotel.*

It had become my custom to begin with a variation on a line from the songwriter Paul Simon: "Here I am Lord, standing at your place of business." Which is what I did this time. What happened next took me by surprise—and by storm.

Words exploded in a silent scream: "You *&%$#, you took my Tali! You *&%$#, you took my Tali!" That explosion took on a life of its own, going on and on and on and on. I didn't know how long it would go, but I knew I had to let it for as long as it needed. After what must have been dozens of repetitions, it stopped. Exhausted, so did I.

I managed to pull myself together and asked for greater understanding in coming to terms with this tragedy. I expressed my gratitude for God's continuing guidance and for the sacred teachings that brought that awareness closer. Finally, I walked away.

On one hand, my outburst made no sense. At whom was I yelling at and why? There's an old joke about that, too. After a rabbi pours out his heart at the *Kotel,* asking for peace and well-being for himself, his family, and the world, a student approaches and asks him what it's like to pray like that. The rabbi replies, "It's like talking to a wall."

---

5. Unattributed quotations are by the author.

Okay, so I was talking to a wall. But what else was I doing? Maybe accusing some ancient or childhood concept of God I still harbored. Maybe taking advantage of a safe place for some much-needed release. Maybe—I didn't know what exactly.

In Judaism, we teach that it is all right to be angry with God—that God has "broad shoulders," that God can "take it," and so on. But that only makes sense if God has purposely harmed us. If God did not take Talia deliberately, if this is not how God acts, then anger like that is misdirected. If God is not the source of our hurt, directing our rage at God is not going to bring us any closer to resolution, or peace.[6]

The second part of my Western Wall encounter was easier to process. I could still express gratitude for the teachings I had made it my business to learn. I could still appreciate the moral guidance they offered. I remained a grateful soul and expected to maintain a relationship with God. But the terms of that relationship needed to change.

6. I do not use the word "closure" in such circumstances. There are many things, and I consider this one of them, that cannot reasonably be expected to "close."

# 2

# Faith: It's Not Easy

## MY GOD IS REAL—MYSTICALLY SO

PEOPLE BECOME RABBIS, PRIESTS, ministers, imams, etc., for a variety of reasons. One of mine was the desire to know and serve God better.

My relationship with God began in earnest when I was a young man, still in college and searching for something. I was not sure what. One day, in an open field, with mother earth below and the sky above, I experienced a feeling of great closeness to what I took to be God's presence. No drugs were involved.

I did not fully comprehend the experience but somehow intuited that it would be a touchstone for my life going forward. I subsequently learned that people describe such experiences as mystical encounters. They have been chronicled in every human culture.

In some ways, the mystical can account for what the rational cannot. When every rational argument for or against God's existence has been made, analyzed, and dispatched, the testimony of mystical experience remains.

So, when like most clergy I've been asked if God really exists, my standard response has been, "I believe so, yes."

But even mystical experience cannot answer all of our questions. It may serve as testimony in favor of God's existence, but it gives no justification for my daughter's, or any other, tragic death.

# WHY FAITH? WHAT GOD?

Many people, especially in the wake of tragedy, not only question their own faith in God but the need for faith in the first place. Others abandon faith altogether. I did not expect that this would happen to me. Living without a higher calling or higher interests strikes me as a poor way to live. If we are going to focus only on what is immediate and tangible—only on our elemental needs and drives—human life becomes essentially indistinguishable from animal life. If civilization is going to ignore our deeper humanity, if it is only going to be guided by survival of the fittest and might makes right, we will degenerate into creatures focused on power, domination, and little else.

Every great faith is built on the understanding that there is more to life than this. A life without higher voices and nobler truths is a life that will likely be small. Faith bestows value on others while it uplifts us. Its teachings guide us to be more deeply and compassionately involved with our fellow human beings, as well as with the animals with whom we share the planet.

The case for faith may be relatively easy to make, but keeping faith alive and real is not so easy. Justice does not always prevail and the righteous suffer as much as anyone. We can understand why so many people these days, when asked for religious affiliation, answer, "None." And people of faith, some-faith and no-faith alike are given to wonder, "What God can possibly be behind all this?"

## THE FAIRNESS CONTRACT

Young children are taught, believe, and even demand, that life should be fair. Most of us, as we grow into adulthood, maintain this same attitude. If we work hard, are honest in our dealings, and show the same respect to others that we want shown to us, we expect to be treated fairly in return. Most people believe that society itself should be structured along these same lines.

We can call this arrangement "the fairness contract." Not coincidentally, it mirrors the terms of the covenant between God and the Israelites in the Hebrew Bible. "If you act justly, I will bless you," more or less sums it up.

At the same time, we know that life does not always work out this way. That fairness contract seems to have an awful lot of loopholes. The "do good and be rewarded" equation often seems out of balance. When it is, our faith is tested. We want to know why that contract is not being better enforced. We also want to know who exactly is supposed to be enforcing it.

It is relatively easy to account for the collective shortcomings of human civilization. Overreaching egos chasing power and fame and exercising misguided will have been wreaking havoc since *homo sapiens* first walked the earth.

Reconciling the fairness contract with the injustices that befall us as individuals is more difficult. If we are going to get through life's unavoidable unfairness with faith intact, we need to better understand the God who purportedly stands behind it.

## GAPS

Before Talia's death, the gap between life as it was and life as a just God would have it, played a relatively minor role in my faith—and my rabbinate. When questions about life's unfairness arose, most often after a congregant's personal tragedy, I would try to redirect the focus to their more immediate needs. Even in retrospect, this seems to have been the wisest course. In times of need, a caring presence is what matters most. Answers can wait, especially if they are going to lead to more difficult questions.

I also believed that if a faith can deal competently with so many of life's complex questions, it should not be rejected if it struggles with a relative few of them.

The testimony I offered at Talia's funeral was true. It was faith that enabled us to raise a daughter such as this. And it did much more. Faith was at the center of our lifelong marriage. Faith allowed me to serve as a spiritual leader, to found and guide a thriving congregation. Faith enabled me to earn a measure of respect from those I respected in return. Faith provided me with equilibrium during life's inevitable ups and downs. Faith grounded my life with purpose and direction.

Life without faith seemed pretty much out of the question. But now I needed either more faith, deeper faith, or a different faith. I needed a faith that could pass the Tragedy Test.

## TEMPLE DESTROYED, FAITH ADAPTS

The Bible records that in the year 586 BCE,[1] after standing for nearly four centuries, King Solomon's Temple—along with much of the capital city, Jerusalem, in which it stood—was destroyed by invading Babylonians. In the wake of the calamity, the Jewish people were exiled from their homeland. Testimony appeared in the Book of Psalms, "By the waters of Babylon, we sat and wept as we remembered Zion."[2]

The refugees from Jerusalem were weeping for many reasons. In addition to the Temple, they had lost loved ones, homes, and much of their way of life. They may have been weeping for a lost God as well. Their ancestral Deity, who promised to protect and preserve them, had evidently not kept that promise. God's own house lay in ruins. Without a functioning Temple, how would they maintain their relationship with God? Without that relationship, how could they survive as a people?

As the people sat and wept, their sages developed new understandings. They proclaimed that the relationship with God would continue, Temple or no. They taught that God could be found everywhere and that God could be served from anywhere. With these and other innovative teachings, the faith of Israel survived.

The destruction of the First Temple was not the last catastrophe in Jewish history. Through the centuries, struggle, exile, and tragedy have been recurrent. When disaster struck, the people wanted to know how and where their just and caring God fit in. Each time, spiritual leaders offered explanations. In the process, new beliefs and understandings came to be.

§

1. Before the Common Era, equivalent to 586 BC.

2. Psalms 137:1.

The faith of individuals can follow a similar track. When life is proceeding normally, people often take their faith for granted and set aside difficult questions. But when things go wrong, we want to know why. We want to know what happened to order, meaning, and justice. We want to know how that fairness contract applies. We want answers from the God who is allegedly in charge.

# 3

# Our Explanations

## EVERYTHING HAPPENS FOR A REASON

THERE ARE PEOPLE OF traditional faith, people of secular faith, and even people who claim to be of no faith, who nonetheless subscribe to a particular affirmation of faith. It is that "everything happens for a reason." The phrase is heard across the faith spectrum, from those who claim to be pious and observant, to those who claim to be agnostic or atheist, and from people who say they are somewhere in between.

An almost primal human desire for order, meaning, and purpose in life—whether we understand that purpose or not—seems to underlie this. "Everything happens for a reason" is an affirmation that a Higher Power somehow guides the universe, ultimately for good. It is reassuring to believe this, especially if our world has been turned upside down.

But in truth, it is much easier to say that everything happens for a reason if the magnitude of the upset is mild to moderate. When a crisis is severe, people are not as quick to repeat it, and rightly so. One would have to be incredibly insensitive to say something like, "I'm sorry your loved one was just diagnosed with terminal cancer, but I believe everything happens for a reason." When the stakes are high, the shortcomings of this popular phrase are exposed. It can readily inflict more pain than comfort. What's more, we don't really know whether it is true in the first place.

# MAYBE IT DOESN'T

Macbeth, in William Shakespeare's play of the same name, offers that things can and do happen for no reason at all. Following the death of his wife he rages,

> "Life's but . . . a tale told by an idiot, full of sound and fury, signifying nothing."[1]

Macbeth is claiming that there is no higher order or master plan, hidden or otherwise. His perspective may not be comforting, but it is not irrational. The world frequently appears as if no one, certainly no responsible adult—to say nothing of a Righteous Judge—is in charge.

Macbeth's argument actually appears in a traditional Jewish source composed more than a thousand years before Shakespeare. A Rabbinic discussion records the assertion that, "There is no judgment and there is no Judge." Although offered by a prominent sage, it is a minority position, directly countered, "There *is* judgment and there *is* a Judge."[2]

In other words, everything, great and small, happens for a reason. This perspective became a pillar of classical Judaism, Christianity, and Islam.

The Rabbis may have considered the likes of Macbeth heretical, but they knew that many people saw the world as he did. Chaos and injustice frequently appear to supersede that fairness contract—for no conceivable reason. It is to their credit that they recorded a view contrary to their own.

So, is there justice and a Judge—or not? Does everything happen for a reason, or is what we see "sound and fury signifying nothing?" Are our lives, as the Book of Ecclesiastes puts it, "emptiness, vanity, and a striving after wind,"[3] or are they somehow infused with higher meaning, even divinity?

---

1. Shakespeare, *Macbeth*, Act 5, Scene 5.
2. *Genesis Rabbah*, 26.
3. Ecclesiastes 2:17.

These are not small questions. The way we answer them will determine, in significant measure, the way we approach life. They can also help us understand—or not—why tragedy befalls people whom we all agree do not deserve it.

We will continue our exploration, as many have before us, with the Book of Job.

## IT IS A MYSTERY

According to the book of the Bible that bears his name, Job was a righteous man: good, noble, and true. He was favored with every worldly blessing: health, family, prosperity, and more. Suddenly, and without earthly explanation, everything is taken from him—children, well-being, wealth.[4] What Job suffers in a short period is far more than most human beings endure in a lifetime.

The Book of Job revolves around the question, "Why does Job suffer?" The subtext is, "Why do we?" The Bible typically claims that people suffer because they disobey God's will, i.e., because they sin. But Job is not your typical biblical book.

As succeeding tragedies befall Job, his friends, in an effort to comfort him, give voice to the traditional view. They tell him he is suffering because he must have done something wrong. With a God who is altogether just, the God in whom they all believed, Job would not be punished unless he somehow deserved it.

Job rejects both his friends' words and the beliefs that inform them. He insists that he has led an upright life and has done nothing that could justify what has befallen him. By maintaining his innocence, Job challenges a foundational biblical principle: disobeying God may indeed cause suffering but that does not mean that the converse is also true. Not all suffering is the result of disobeying God.

This is not a small point, and we can embrace it. But it does not resolve our larger question. If Job has done nothing to deserve it, *especially* if he has done nothing to deserve it, why is he suffering in the first place?

Job and his friends wrangle over this question for thirty-odd chapters and fail to resolve the issue. Ultimately, the Almighty appears, and the multi-sided conversation becomes a monologue. Literally and figuratively, God blows everyone away.

---

4. Actually, Job is suffering because God and Satan made a bet. (Job 1:11–12) But this is generally understood as a literary device used to introduce the ensuing questions.

Out of a whirlwind-tempest-cyclone, God belittles human attempts to comprehend such matters. The Almighty thunders, "Where were you when I made heaven and earth?"[5] As if to say, "How can you even pretend to understand the workings and mysteries of My Creation?" According to the Book of Job, the suffering of the righteous is a mystery beyond our ability to solve.

This whirlwind explanation—that there is a reason we do not understand—falls short in many ways. It is less an explanation than a show of force. It silences more than it explains. We could call it "shock and awe" theology. God is saying that the reason good people suffer is, like the whirlwind itself, impenetrable.

We can take this as an improvement over the theology of Job's friends, who believed that inexplicable suffering must somehow be a consequence of disobeying God's will. The book allows us to conclude that sin and suffering are not, necessarily and always, cause and effect. It is a source of comfort for this very reason. The Sages are to be commended for including it in the biblical canon.

The Book of Job also reminds us of our own limitations alongside God's boundless power. But we have no greater understanding of the reasons behind human suffering at the end of the book than we did at the beginning.

§

For the moment, let's accept this. Many of us had a difficult enough time with high school physics, which was child's play compared to the metaphysics of misfortune. For all of our advanced knowledge in so many fields, when it comes to the question of divine justice, or lack thereof, our understanding remains minuscule.

Even today, endless mysteries great and small remain. We know far less about subjects such as love, beauty, nature, friendship, and peace, to name but a few, than we wish we did. If we cannot fathom these, why should we expect to be able to answer what may be the greatest mystery of all—the suffering of the righteous

5. Job 38:4.

and the flourishing of the wicked in a world ostensibly overseen by a just God?

The Book of Job has been counseling us to accept this lack of understanding for 2500 years. We acknowledge that it is better to admit we do not understand something than it is to pretend that we do. Especially in the realm of faith, a healthy sense of humility can keep us from reaching false conclusions. Knowledge to stay away from error is critical knowledge.

Still, most of us don't like being told that something is beyond us, especially something as important as this. So our search continues.

## PERHAPS WE CAN SOLVE IT

"Has It Ever Occurred to You That You Might Be Wrong?"[6]

—SNOOPY

Few of us would tell our friends what Job's friends told him—that he was suffering because he sinned. First of all, it is presumptuous. They had no evidentiary grounds to assume it. We would also consider it rude. Besides, since the divine law is quite extensive, it is difficult for anyone to say they have not broken at least some portion of it.

Speaking personally, while Lord knows I am guilty of much, I can say with equal assurance that I have done nothing so egregious, even in sum, to deserve the death of my daughter. The same obviously goes for Talia herself. The scales are far too out of balance to argue that her death was a pure expression of divine justice.

Job's friends are not only being harsh, they are not being credible. We've all seen far too many innocent people hurt to say that sin and guilt must be the default explanation when things go wrong.

Yet people continue to say that everything happens for a reason. And they generally mean more than smoking causes heart disease, fire destroys property, or drunk drivers cause accidents. The popular phrase implies that metaphysics and morality are inextricably involved.

§

This is not all that different from God's message to Job and his friends. God says we should not expect to understand what happened to Job, but at the same time intimates that it happened for a reason. The reason may be hidden from us, but there is a reason nonetheless.

6. Announcing the title of his book on theology. Schultz, *Beagles and Bunnies,* back cover.

The belief that God has a reason is reason enough for many of us. It goes along with the belief that God is all-just and all-powerful. If it happened, there must have been a reason—and a good one—whether we can conceive of what that reason might be or not.

If this is your faith, and you do not want it disturbed, you may want to put the book down here, or give it to a friend. I promise I will not be insulted. Faith and belief are highly personal. We are also in a realm where no one can say that they know for certain. The explanation in Job was not sufficient for me. I needed to look further. Perhaps you do, too.

## IF FOR NO REASON—THEN WHY?

If everything happens for some higher reason, the corollary is that nothing happens for no reason. That, too, is a widely held belief. The many conspiracy theories surrounding the assassination of President John F. Kennedy illustrate the point. Each of them feeds on the sense that there simply had to be more than a lone, pathetic gunman involved. Even though the best evidence we possess suggests that this was, in fact, the case.

We yearn for both empirical truth and emotional solace. When they are in conflict, we often find it easier to configure the facts to fit our theories than the other way around.

It is understandable. If everything does indeed happen for a reason, it means there is at least some transcendent significance to our loss. But this belief comes with a high price tag. Carried to its logical end, it means that God has deliberately chosen to inflict pain and suffering upon us.

Is that really preferable to the idea that our great personal tragedy was an empty, random, or meaningless happenstance? Apparently for some people it is.

I do not believe that Talia's death was the result of a deliberate action by God. Nor can I fathom, much less worship, any God who would have so decided to take her life. So, the question remains: how could it have happened?

# 4

# Faith for Difficult Times

"I've often been asked if religious faith isn't just a crutch.
Yes it is, I would answer.
Now what makes you think you aren't limping?"[1]
—REV. WILLIAM SLOANE COFFIN

IN ANCIENT DAYS, PEOPLE would often explain tragedy as the will of the gods or as the consequence of an improperly offered sacrifice. Over time, those morphed into, "It is God's will" or "God is testing us." Today people suggest, "God doesn't give people more than they can handle," "It was meant to be," "Everything happens for a reason," and "It will be made right in heaven."

People don't, and didn't, say these things because we know them to be true. We know nothing of the sort. People say them because we *want* them to be true. People say them because we are desperate for every drop of comfort and meaning we can get. We say them because we refuse to allow that human life, particularly our own lives and the lives of our loved ones, may have been in vain, even, or especially, when they end tragically. We say them because there is little more terrifying than random horror, and we

1. Speech at Cornell University, early 1970s. Related by Prof. Alan Fischler, PhD.

31

don't cherish the prospect of living in a world where that is the norm.

In the closing scene of the classic movie *Casablanca,* Rick (Humphrey Bogart) utters the famous words: ". . . it doesn't take much to see that the problems of three little people don't amount to a hill of beans in this crazy world." He is, of course, correct—they don't. In this crazy world, there are many things that come before our own happiness. In *Casablanca,* it was war. In our personal lives, it can be a tragedy.

Even if we understand this intellectually, it remains psychologically and spiritually unsettling. It is one of the reasons we turn to one another in times of loss. Human relationships reassure us that in the presence of the worst, we still matter. Even Rick in *Casablanca* turns to his longtime frenemy Louis to begin "a beautiful friendship."

We turn to faith for the same reason. It reminds us that we are important. It can give us reassurance. It can even put us in the presence of the most important presence of all, the presence of God.

## SERIOUSLY, LIFE CAN BE ABSURD

Long before the famous movie came out, I was a fan of Ground-hog Day, the day. It has been my favorite American holiday since I was a teenager. First of all, it was no one else's. (Thanksgiving? Independence Day? How trite.) Second, like most adolescents, I was looking for a way to stand out from the crowd. I suppose this all could have been avoided if I had made the football team, but that didn't happen.

Anyway, it was harmless enough. Every year on February 2nd, I would wish people a "Happy Groundhog Day." The day before I would encourage them to have a nice Groundhog Day. The day after I would ask if they had a good Groundhog Day. (Don't you wish you knew me then?) I kept this up well into adulthood.

One year, on the evening of February 2nd, while waiting for the high school students in my Confirmation class to filter in, I was chitchatting with the early arrivals about, what else, Ground-hog Day. I thought it was clear that I was being playful, but one of the students took it more seriously than I'd intended. Out came the question: "Rabbi, why do you care so much about Groundhog Day?"

I needed an answer that preserved my credibility and made sense—fast. Out of my mouth came, "I like Groundhog Day because it celebrates the absurd." The students got it, and loved it.

Why wouldn't they? Life in high school is nothing if not absurd. For that matter, the same can be said for much of life as an adult. The choice is to either go mad or to have some fun along the way. Groundhog Day takes something absurd—a long-term weather prediction from an oversized rodent emerging from hibernation—and pokes fun at us all in the process.[2]

Groundhogs aside, absurdity is a serious challenge for people of faith. It mocks our attempts to make sense of the world. Random tragedy can find its way to any of us. And its impact can be too serious for us to shake our heads and laugh.

---

2. I realize there are also quasi-sacred origins to the customs of Ground-hog Day and I mean no disrespect. See Elliott, *What About the Groundhog?*

In Voltaire's eighteenth-century novel, *Candide*, the *dramatis personae* travel the globe and witness a full complement of humanity's horrors. Through it all, one of them, Professor Pangloss, declares that they live in "the best of all possible worlds."[3] Talk about absurd.[4]

*Candide* concludes (spoiler alert) with the words, "Tend your garden." It seems to be Voltaire's way of saying that, in the face of a world that can be ridiculous, shallow, and violent, the best course may be to live a life of productive domesticity.

This is not the only possible response to the wider world's absurdity, but it is an appealing one. It can be easier to find satisfaction focusing on relatively narrow and personal concerns than on national and global ones.

Absurdity was also central to the work of the twentieth-century philosopher Albert Camus. He wrote:

> " . . . the absurd arises when the human need to understand meets the unreasonableness of the world, when my appetite for the absolute and for unity meets the impossibility of reducing this world to a rational and reasonable principle."[5]

Many of us have that appetite for the absolute and for unity, but no one has yet put forth a rational and reasonable principle that accounts for the meaninglessness we so often encounter. There is no unified field theory that explains it all—neither in physics nor in metaphysics. In the absence of such a theory, we are left to conclude that some things make sense while others are, in fact, absurd.

Aside from staying home and tending our garden (which may reduce, but will not eliminate, the possibility of random tragedy), there are other ways to cope with this reality. We can express ourselves artistically and creatively. We can become more resilient. We can strengthen our sense of humor. We can learn to engage the world on its terms.

3. Voltaire, *Candide*, 40.

4. Pangloss is generally taken to be a caricature of the German philosopher Baron Gottfried W. Leibniz (1646–1716) who taught a similar doctrine.

5. Camus, *Myth of Sisyphus*, Myth 28.

We can also attempt to live a life grounded in deeper values. We can practice kindness, work to repair the world or otherwise pursue a life of service.

People of faith call these paths holy. Building a life that is, in the greatest possible measure, not absurd, can help keep the sense that life is futile at the greatest possible distance. It can also help us better deal with the absurdity of the injustice when tragedy finds us.

Still, our craving for deeper understanding remains.

## MONOTHEISM, POLYTHEISM, AND ATHEISM

Polytheistic idolatry dominated religious life in the centuries before, and even after, the God of Abraham arrived on the scene. There is little mystery in polytheism. If there is rain, it is because the god of rain willed it. If there is fertility, the god of fertility must have willed that. If there is chaos, the gods were fighting, etc. Polytheists did not expect much in the way of justice from the gods. They believed they acted as recklessly as humans—with all of the attendant consequences.

Ethical Monotheism looks at life differently. It holds that the one God demands justice of us and, if we are faithful, we have the right to expect the same in return.

It is clear that when we act justly, it does shape life and society for the better. The belief that God executes justice on our behalf is more problematic. We remain painfully aware of the disparity between what is and what ought to be.

But the monotheistic faiths are not considered great because they are simple. They are considered great because they challenge us—and through these challenges, we grow.

§

Few people believe in polytheism today. Even faiths that offer multiple representations of God allow that the many faces are actually manifestations of the greater One.

We may tell ourselves that we have evolved from our polytheistic roots and that monotheism is a superior understanding of the nature of the divine. But we may not be fully evolved as monotheists either. When confronted with an unjust outcome, the ancient polytheists would say, "It is the will of the gods." Many of us say, "It is God's will." The difference is not great.

§

Injustice and tragedy are likewise easy for an atheist to explain. If there is no God, there is no expectation of divine justice—and fewer agonized questions in the wake of misfortune. We've already seen Macbeth's claim that, "Life's but . . . a tale told by an idiot, full of sound and fury, signifying nothing." Shakespeare renders our existential frustration with precision. Who among us has not weighed the thought, especially in the aftermath of a tragedy, that life has no higher significance—to say nothing of higher justice?

A polytheist can understand life's sound and fury as the result of the many gods' machinations. A traditional monotheist might understand it as the inscrutable will of the one God. An atheist can say it is just the way things are.

Both the polytheist and atheist understandings of God are rational. They provide straightforward answers to our complicated questions. If there is no Supreme Being or Force for Good that guides or wills events, then there is no reason to be confounded in the wake of a disaster. There is nothing to complain about and no one to complain to.

Monotheists reject this view. This is not because it doesn't seem true—oft times it seems all too true. We reject it because it gives us nowhere to turn. We reject it because we refuse to accept that our lives signify nothing. Whatever truth there may be in polytheism, atheism or Macbeth's piercing words, they do not give most of us enough of the existential strength we need to navigate our way through life.

Monotheism does not deny that the injustice, chaos, or sound and fury are real. But it challenges the despair to which polytheism and atheism point. Monotheism is not focused on lamenting what is. It is about embracing what might be.

People often give up on monotheism, and God, because of the world's many injustices. To do so is to miss the point. Monotheism does not countenance resignation. It says that injustices are to be challenged—and it outlines in considerable detail how to do so.

However meaningless the sound and fury may appear, the life of an active monotheist remains one of ever-present meaning—and of ever-present struggle to create more of it. This challenge is one of faith's great gifts.

§

A monotheist can also believe that God's power is not the power to make the world just. God's power is the power to inspire us to do so. God's power is the power to make us understand that what is, is not (yet) what ought to be. God's power added to ours is the power to move the world towards justice and righteousness. God's power is the power that gives us the strength to live *as if* we can make a difference, not as if it is pointless to try.

God's power enables us to look at the world with more hope than fear. Life can be frightening. This makes belief in a God that is a force for goodness, comfort, and sustenance vital—especially in the face of great loss.

It is difficult enough to build a just world when people believe it is what God wants us to do. It becomes even more difficult without the motivation that belief gives us. Faith in the one God who demands goodness goes hand in hand with our own commitment to demand goodness. We recognize that there will be inexplicable and unjustifiable exceptions. But if we are going to believe in any God, the One who is our partner in redeeming the world may be the best one we can hope to serve.

The flaws of this worldview are exposed when the righteous suffer, the wicked prosper, and the good die young. When that happens, we need a faith that asks more from us, not less. We need a faith that can respond to the inscrutable and the absurd. Monotheistic faith does not ask us to ignore what we see. It calls upon us to find a way to pass the Tragedy Test.

# 5

# God's Justice—Where?

## CORNERSTONE BIBLICAL PRINCIPLES— VIOLATED

GOD'S SILENCING RESPONSE TO Job and his friends does not much help us in this regard. It does not satisfy our desire for greater understanding. On the contrary, it stokes it. The belief that the reason for a tragedy may be hidden, but that there *is* a reason behind it, has serious ramifications. Applying it personally, it means that God took my daughter for a reason—a reason I may not understand, but a God-intentioned reason nonetheless.

If this is true—if there is a God who ended Talia's life for a given reason, or set of reasons, whatever those reasons might be, there is no way I can continue in relationship with this God. There is no moral rationale, earthly, mysterious, or otherwise, that I can accept as a justification for God willing her death.[1]

The sanctity of human life and the application of justice are central biblical principles. Humanity and God alike are supposed to be bound by them. God commands Moses, "Do what is right

---

1. For many people of faith, belief in an afterlife provides an explanation. We will examine this concept shortly.

and good."[2] In turn, Abraham demands of God, "Shall not the Judge of all the Earth do justly?"[3] Given such a standard, what could possibly justify the taking of this, or any other, innocent human life?

Like every human being, Tali was not without her shortcomings—though I daresay they were few. But there was nothing in her life that even remotely warranted a death sentence from on high.

Traditionalists counter that God may have wanted to punish us, force us to grow or instill in us some deeper appreciation for life's blessings. I find none of these explanations acceptable. If death was the punishment and no capital crime was committed, then the sentence is either disproportionate, illegitimate, or both. We would not accept such a verdict from an earthly court, much less the heavenly one.

If the intention was to somehow "bless" us by making us grow through our sorrow, the Power in question is likewise out of line. Nothing in this world can heal the hurt, soothe the pain, or replace the love of a life taken from us. To say nothing of the injustice done to Tali herself.

Claiming that the undeserved death of a loved one is somehow for our own good perverts everything that faith teaches about the sanctity of human life. If it was, in fact, deliberately brought about by some Higher Power, it means that Power is perverse as well.

Unlike in war, where one side or the other may be fighting for a just cause, and casualties can be understood as the sacrifice of the few for the sake of the many, Tali died for no higher purpose. She was struck by a motor vehicle while jogging.

When natural disasters strike and innocent lives are lost, people wonder how God could do this and what kind of God is acting here?[4] In these situations, too, we search for moral justification—in vain.

2. Deuteronomy 6:18.

3. Genesis 18:25.

4. Even insurance companies suggest that such calamities are "acts of God."

This is not to say that we cannot derive some goodness from Talia's death, as well as from the example she set during her all-too-short life. But to suggest that this was the *reason* God took her implies that God violated cardinal biblical principles in order to get us to do so.

§

We could easily say that by carrying out such a sentence, the God in question is demonstrating an acute deficiency in judgment. Whatever the particulars, a God who takes innocent lives for such mysterious or hidden reasons is not a God that someone who has lost a loved one can be compelled to hold holy.

Many of the ancients believed that good harvests, fertility, military success, and the like were granted by their gods in exchange for human sacrifice. The God of the Bible was supposed to be different. In place of human sacrifice, the God of the Bible asks for righteousness. Instead of cruelty, the God of the Bible demands justice and love.

Our ideas of God have evolved through history. But if we continue to maintain that in his[5] own inscrutable way God takes innocent lives, we have not traveled very far from our polytheistic forebears and their merciless idols. We need a God who can pass the Tragedy Test, not one who fails it and doubles down on, or flaunts, the failure.

---

5. For the sake of linguistic convenience I am making use of the male pronoun. God, of course, transcends gender. But the use of a gender-based pronoun, whatever it might be, highlights one of the difficulties we encounter when we assign various human characteristics to God, e.g., personality, emotion, senses, etc. More on this shortly.

## DOES GOD LAUGH?

The Bible has the official word on God's actions, but a popular Yiddish folk saying offers an alternative view: "We plan and God laughs." The modern writer Shalom Auslander has suggested that if this is true, it makes God a punk.[6]

Auslander is being irreverent but he is not being illogical. If God is up there laughing at our plans and pulling strings to foil them, then punk is, in fact, a fitting description. It means that no matter how sincerely we labor to fulfill our dreams, we know that at any moment God may "laugh," and they will be shattered.

But the phrase "God laughs" is not necessarily meant to suggest that God is out to get us. Rather, it is a way of expressing frustration that the universe can be demonstrably indifferent to even our most worthy efforts, hopes, and dreams. It is a statement of resignation that at the end of the day, the world, and whatever God may be in it, cannot be counted on to keep us from undeserved harm, pain, or sorrow—much less to tilt the table in our direction.

6. Auslander, *New York Times*, May 11, 2012

## IT HAPPENS TO PEOPLE LIKE US, TOO

As a congregational rabbi, one of my duties was to counsel people who were coping with tragedy. Because they were often people who tried to be—and frequently were—good, they were often shocked when "things like this" happened to "people like us."

Living rightly has much to recommend it, and it is, without doubt, the way to live. But as the saying goes, expecting life to treat you fairly because you are a good person is like expecting the bull not to charge you because you are a vegetarian.

It is an inescapable fact that calamity happens to people who do not deserve it. As even a Talmudic commentary notes, "There is death without sin and suffering without wrongdoing."[7] Misfortune can strike even the best people for no reason. A living faith needs to account for this.

Still, with all the evidence to the contrary, many of us prefer to live as if a benevolent and all-powerful God watches over and protects us. Emotionally, it can be comforting. Psychologically, it can be a defense mechanism. All along, we may be fooling ourselves.

---

7. *Tosafot, Berachot* 46b.

## AFTERLIFE?

While counseling grieving families, I would, on occasion, mention the possibility of an afterlife. This was not because I was certain there is one, but because I knew that for some the thought would be comforting.

Belief in an afterlife is also a way to maintain faith in a God who is just. If we do not see justice in this world, perhaps we will see it in the next.

I, too, comforted myself with belief in an afterlife in the days following Tali's death. I told myself, and others, that she was alive and well in the next world and that I would see her again one day—loving and smiling as she was at her best. Soon enough, I came to understand that was my grief talking. I was telling myself something I needed to hear, not something I knew to be true. This realization was disquieting. But I could not pretend otherwise.

## SO IS GOD ALWAYS JUST?

Theodicy is the branch of philosophy that attempts to justify God's actions.[8] It refuses to accept that God acts unjustly. When bad conduct seems to be rewarded, or when good conduct is not, believers in theodicy—and they are found in many faiths—look for ways to justify God's apparent behavior.

In the Bible itself, however, God's judgments are often challenged. Abraham argues that it is wrong for God to destroy Sodom's righteous along with its wicked. Moses protests God's judgment against the Israelites. Jeremiah complains that the wicked prosper.[9] No matter. Believers in theodicy defend God's reported actions, whatever they might be.

Some will cite as a prooftext the verse from *Psalms*, "God's judgments are true and righteous altogether."[10] Others contend that evil is a construct of our minds, and if we release our attachments to life's duality, we will overcome suffering. And again, there are those who claim that every injustice in this world will be set right by God in the next one.

Each of these, and similar, related beliefs, have their adherents. The preeminent twelfth-century Jewish philosopher Moses Maimonides appears to reject them. He teaches that evil, and the injustice that stems from it, is either wrought by nature, by other people, or is self-inflicted.[11] Note that God is missing from the equation altogether.

---

8. From the Greek *Theos* meaning "God" and *dikē*, "judgment." The discipline came to prominence in the eighteenth century.

9. Genesis 18:23; Exodus 32:31 and others; Jeremiah 12:1.

10. Psalms 19:10.

11. Maimonides, *Guide for the Perplexed*, III:12.

## FROM THE KABBALAH

The school of Jewish mysticism, known as Kabbalah, deals with the issue of injustice as well. Kabbalists believe that during Creation, God contracted into himself in an action known as *tsimtsum*. This process allowed chaos to fill the spaces where God was more fully present prior to that act of contraction. Where God is fully present, there is no injustice. In the places from which God has withdrawn, opposition forces of evil and injustice can fill the vacuum.

Why God would do such a thing in the first place is another question. Perhaps to give us the opportunity to fill those empty spaces with goodness, love, and justice. In any case, the doctrine of *tsimtsum* resolves that injustice, accident, and evil occur only where God is less than fully present. It is an ingenious response to the metaphysical problem of why the innocent suffer in a world purportedly ruled by a just God.

This Kabbalistic philosophy recognizes that there are order and meaning, as well as evil and tragedy, in the universe. It does not attempt to justify injustice or even to say that God intended for it to happen. It simply affirms that there are matters beyond God's self-contracted reach.

This idea that God is less present in some places than others can also be found in Rabbinic teachings. A verse in the book of Isaiah states, "You are my Witnesses, says God."[12] A commentary offers, "When you are my witnesses, I am God; when you are not, it is as if I am not God."[13] In other words, God is absent when people fail to ensure that God is sufficiently present.

This Kabbalistic idea of God may be a construct, but it is more sophisticated than many we find in the Bible. It gives us a God who is benevolent, but places responsibility for the state of humanity on us. It responds to tragedy by saying that not even God, having self-limited, can prevent it.

12. Isaiah 43:12

13 *Sifrei* Deuteronomy 346.

It is a theory that is intellectually coherent. The God it describes may even pass the Tragedy Test. But it will strike many of us as contrived. Like all theodicy, this teaching of Kabbalah is determined to come to a particular conclusion—that God simply must be all-just.

## WHEN WE SEE GOD AS PERSONAL

"God sat out the Holocaust—
but you expect him on your side for the big game?"

Many religious traditions assure us that God grants our requests when we merit them.[14] Even if part of us questions whether God really acts in this way, we may find it psychologically, even existentially, comforting to believe it. We want God's help in securing the things that matter most to us.

Theologians describe the God of whom we make such requests as a personal God, i.e., a God we conceive of as having at least some of the characteristics of a person. We may ask our personal God to help us earn a living, to heal an illness, to right an injustice, even to help our team score touchdowns.

Though we know from experience that asking God to do such things rarely changes external outcomes, we do it anyway. We continue even after it becomes clear that if the personal God is listening, he does not care—at least not enough to intervene. The personal God either does not or cannot put his thumb on the scale and tip it towards deserved goodness and away from undeserved misfortune—certainly not in any reliable fashion.

Most of us realize that the laws of the universe are not going to be altered in our favor simply because we've asked God nicely. We may even appreciate that it is an absurd conceit to think this. Yet, we ask anyway. Probably because it is comforting to believe that the world works in this fashion—at least sometimes. Life is difficult, and we are grateful for whatever help we can get from wherever we think we can get it.

So we continue to ask our personal God for favors, great and small. But when this personal God does not respond to even our most sincere and desperate pleas, we may seriously question whether God acts this way at all. And if we conclude that God doesn't, the next question may be whether or not God is real in the first place.

14. See, for example, Psalms 145:19.

§

There are those who say that God's apparent non-responsiveness is not a reason to question God's existence. If our heartfelt prayers are not granted, perhaps this is because God answered, "No." But this, too, is problematic.

Agricultural tribes throughout history would sing, pray, and dance, imploring God, or the gods, to make it rain. Aware of what was at stake, they did so with as much devotion as they could muster.

Still, their prayers were not always answered, at least not affirmatively. Crops would fail, animals would starve, and people would die. A skeptic might say, there is no God. A believer might say, God said no.

There is, of course, another possibility, and it is that God is not in the business of making it rain on request in the first place. Perhaps our personal pleas, however sincere, have nothing to do with whether it rains or not. Rain comes when nature warrants it—prayers or no prayers. Most moderns accept this. But we continue to put our personal requests before God anyway.

We live with many such spiritual ambiguities and contradictions, consciously and subconsciously. It may be better to have a relationship with God based on flawed premises than to have no relationship at all. We might even say that such belief is relatively harmless.

But it is only harmless until it isn't. If the God to whom we pray favors goodness and righteousness, we will be shocked to discover that this favor does not extend to the situations that matter to us most, e.g., the lives of our loved ones. If we are struck by an unjust calamity, our spiritual foundation will be rocked. Our personal God will fail the Tragedy Test—at the worst possible time and in the worst possible way.

When that time comes, many people lose their faith. Others become embittered, alienated, or depressed. This need not be the case. Perhaps it is possible for us to understand God in a different manner altogether.

## BELIEFS: TRUE AND NECESSARY

To help with this, we return to Maimonides, the medieval philosopher and legalist. He taught that the Bible contains two kinds of beliefs: true and necessary. He offers as an example of the former that God is eternal. An example of the latter is that God executes perfect justice. Maimonides describes this belief as necessary because it facilitates the maintenance of civic order and it helps to avoid social chaos.[15]

Every great religion teaches that God is caring, loving, powerful, and protecting. Are these beliefs necessary or true? The belief that a personal God loves and cares for us can be comforting and supporting. At the same time, we have all seen enough undeserved suffering to recognize that this belief is only intermittently true, at best.

Many of us have a faith that consists at least partially of necessary beliefs. There is nothing wrong with this. But as we make our way through life, we may come to junctures where we realize that those necessary beliefs are not as true as we wish they were.

15. The distinction between necessary and true beliefs can be found in Maimonides' *Guide for the Perplexed*, III:28. The idea of God as eternal is in the *Guide* beginning in I:1. You can read more about Maimonides' life and thought in many works.

## INSISTING ON A PERSONAL GOD ANYWAY

Logical considerations notwithstanding, there are many reasons why we may not be eager to relinquish our hold on a personal God. A personal God can be both accessible and understandable. Belief in a God who protects us can give us some of the armor we need to face a hostile world.

An additional reason has been outlined by the Israeli scholar Micah Goodman. Goodman has written that people have a need to be noticed by others, particularly those who are greater than we are.[16]

We recognize the phenomenon. Whenever famous, powerful, wealthy, popular, glamorous, or otherwise prominent people bestow attention upon us, we feel flattered, appreciated, and perhaps even validated. Throughout the world, societies, hierarchies, and power structures are built on this understanding.

People of faith also want to be noticed—by God. This may be how the belief that God takes note of everything we do became an almost universal religious principle.

This belief is not without its benefits. If God is indeed mindful of the particulars of our lives, it can motivate us to imbue them with greater goodness and significance.

But Maimonides and other philosophers consider the idea that God pays personal attention to each of us illogical. If God did so, they argue, it would violate God's unchanging and perfect unity. And of course, the fact that ruin comes to good people and success comes to bad ones likewise refutes the notion that a just God personally protects us—at least in this world.

16. Goodman, *Sodotav*, 90.

## WHY WE NEED MORE

Even taking all of these questions, doubts, and inadequate answers into account, maintaining a relationship with a personal God is not without its beauties. It can provide a relatively easy entry into the world of faith. It can put us on relational terms with a Higher Power, which we can then invite into our lives at moments great and small. It can reinforce the connection between us and the divine. It can remind us that we are not in this world for ourselves alone, and that life has a greater and higher purpose.

At the same time, a relationship with a personal God has fundamental shortcomings. A God we can address in personal terms is a God who is, by definition, small. A personal God does not satisfactorily answer the question, "Why?" And plead though we may, our personal God does not keep us safe from life's storms.

If our God is a personal one, we will be doubly distraught when we face misfortune—by the calamity itself and by our God's failure to protect us from it.

Every religious tradition has responses to such situations. We have already seen that they include, "it is for some inscrutable reason," "to teach us a lesson," and "we must have been found wanting in some way that was important to God." Are such answers worthy of a God who insists on our unconditional love and devotion? For many people, the answer is no. So we continue to wonder. If God is neither personal nor just, what are we to make of the countless stories and prayers that describe him as such?

# 6

# Holy Words

"For Rosie, who didn't believe a word of this."[1]
—BOOKPLATE INSCRIPTION,
*THE FIVE BOOKS OF MOSES*

## FROM NARRATIVE: OUR VALUES

EVERYONE LOVES A GOOD story, or as we may also call it, a narrative. We like to tell stories because they help us make sense of the world around us. Life lived in real time can seem random and disconnected. Narrative can give it order, and often, meaning. Whether we are happy or horrified, confused or outraged, narratives help us put life in perspective.

Ever since language first evolved, people have been sharing narratives. Coffee and cocktail conversation can be narrative. Novels are narrative. Political commentary is narrative. Much of the Bible is narrative, too.

Narrative can also play a defining role in a culture. The story of George Washington confessing to cutting down the cherry tree is an American narrative. Santa Claus bringing toys to good girls

---

1. In the sanctuary of the Keys Jewish Community Center, Tavernier, Florida.

and boys is a Christian narrative. Abraham smashing the idols in his father's shop is a Jewish narrative. Although each of these narratives is more legendary than factual, we continue to share them—for a number of good reasons.

The George Washington story is intended to teach that honesty is a fundamental American virtue. Christian children learn about Santa Claus to encourage them to be good. Jews tell the story of Abraham smashing idols to keep people from idolatry.[2] Whether the faith we are talking about is religious or secular, people use narrative to communicate essential values.

---

2. Interestingly, this Jewish legend is presented as an historical occurrence in the *Qur'an, Surah* 21.

## STORIES ARE POWERFUL

The bestselling novel *Life of Pi* details two different accounts of a single shipwreck. In the main telling, the narrator Pi survives, along with a zoo tiger, who, for some reason, has not attacked and killed him. In the second version, a series of natural calamities takes everyone's life except Pi's. Since he is the only witness, neither account can be verified. In the end, police investigators decide they prefer the miraculous story to the conventional one because, "It is the better story." Pi responds, "And so it goes with God."[3]

*Pi*'s author Yann Martel offers that his novel can be summarized in three statements: "Life is a story; you can choose your story; a story with God is the better story."[4]

It is true that people often prefer narratives that tell a better story, even when they don't account for all the facts.

The movie *A Few Good Men* (1992) tells about two U.S. Marines accused of murder on an American military base. As their trial reaches its climax, the prosecutor demands the truth from the commanding officer, played by actor Jack Nicholson. The officer explodes, "You want the truth? You can't handle the truth!" The line has become one of modern cinema's best known. When the truth becomes too difficult to handle, many of us prefer, and will accept, a more reassuring story; we'll deal with the facts later, if at all.

According to literary scholar Jonathan Gottschall,

> " . . . nations tell [stories] about themselves [that] are full of inaccuracies, mostly fiction, not history. These stories accomplish the same function as religion: defining groups, coordinating behavior, and suppressing

3. Martel, *Life of Pi,* 352.
4. Renton, "Yann Martel Interview," Textualities.net.

selfishness in favor of cooperation. Our national myths tell us that not only are we the good guys, but that we are the smartest, boldest, best guys that ever were."[5]

Such stories can be powerful and effective—until we no longer believe them.

5. Gottschall, *Storytelling Animal*, 123.

## RELIGIOUS STORIES ESPECIALLY

Religious stories work similarly. They outline our relationship with God and portray the faithful as favored and elite. They can contain mythical reassurances as well as lasting truths. Often the two are interwoven. As with many nationalist myths, we may believe them until we no longer can.

It is an oft-told religious story that God is not only the most potent force in the universe, but is also altogether good, caring and just.

Perhaps that story acquired as much currency as it did because we know how selfish, violent, and destructive human beings can be when left to their own devices. Belief in a God who holds the guilty accountable might help us overcome some of our baser instincts. Maimonides would describe this as a necessary belief. It may be a better story than the one that says things can happen for no reason at all. It may, in fact, be a story we need to hear—but sooner or later we begin to perceive the holes in it.

People reject nationalist myths when they lead their countries into unjust or self-destructive wars. People reject religious myths when they point to a God who is not credible, to say nothing of cruel, hurtful, or unfair. When the stories break down under the evidence of experience or reason, we need to find new ways to handle those difficult truths.

§

We have also been told the religious story that God asks us to be more than we are and more than we have been. We have been told that serving the God who asks this of us will elevate our lives and enable us to become better people. We have been told that pursuing a life of holiness through learning, service, and humility will elevate the years of our earthly existence.

This story is true—a life and faith can be built on it. It will not disappoint, mislead, or betray us. Admittedly, it does not answer every question we have about God. It remains, however, worthy of a place at the center of a faith worth living. It can even help us with the Tragedy Test.

## THE STORY OF THE BIBLE

For many centuries the narrative sections of the Bible were considered to be both factual and historical—given by God and transmitted by prophet. But scholars have long since concluded that much of biblical history is legendary—the creation of human beings. It is a narrative that delivers the message that the God of Israel is the world's ultimate power and judge.

If we accept that the Bible's narrative portions are the product of human authors, what of its legal codes, its poetry and song? Are they the product of God and prophet, or of ordinary, if gifted, human beings? If we intend to take the Bible seriously, we need to distinguish between the values and teachings that are eternal and those of a particular narrative.

Many biblical verses point us towards a life that is ethical and even holy. These include the injunctions to love your neighbor as yourself, to protect those who are powerless, and to set aside days devoted to pursuits other than work.[6] Others, such as the designation of a subservient role for women, prohibiting the descendants of illegitimate unions from entering the covenant community, and the authorization of mass slaughter are not so elevating.[7]

The classical commentators often attempted to soften or reinterpret some of these harsher dictates. But they remain in the Bible for all to see, a testament to a moral standard much different than our own.

§

Not until the Renaissance did reformist thinkers and scholars in Judaism and Christianity openly question the Bible's claim of divine authorship. In the process, they were often accused of heresy—a serious charge. Possibly with an eye towards mitigating such threats, some of them offered that the Bible was "divinely

6. Leviticus 19:18; Deuteronomy 24:17; Exodus 20:8, *et al.*

7. Genesis 3:16; Deuteronomy 23:2; Numbers 31:7–18, Joshua 6:21, Ezekiel 9:5–6.

inspired." The term was inexact enough to keep at least some religious authorities at bay.

By modern times, Westerners were no longer afraid to say that the books of the Bible were human creations. They have been described as no more divine than the works of Shakespeare, Rembrandt, Mozart, and lesser mortals.

So if the Bible was written, even in part, by fallible human beings—there is of course no other kind—how does that impact our understanding of Scripture and our understanding of God? If our sacred narratives are not divinely authored or even "divinely inspired," what is the source of their authority?

The Bible is the Western world's foundational spiritual text. If that text is largely, if not entirely, the product of human beings—subject to all of the limitations, foibles, and cultural prejudices we know human beings to be—then the Bible is, in essence, a particular narrative. More precisely, it is a particular narrative that carries a particular understanding of a particular God.

If we accept this, we will see the Bible through a much different lens than we would if it were the unquestioned, eternally valid, Word of God.

§

This is a critical point because, as we have seen, it can be an uphill struggle for the Bible's God to pass the Tragedy Test. But if our understanding of that God derives from human storytellers, it does not necessarily mean that God has failed us. It may only mean that the God presented in a particular narrative has.

At the same time, it does not mean that faith fails in its response to some of life's most difficult questions. It does mean that if our faith has left us disappointed, we might do well to look at both God, and what we have been taught is God's Word, through a different lens.

## THE NARRATIVE EVOLVES

Much of the Bible's narrative, its account of history, several of its laws, and any number of its depictions of God have been considered problematic for centuries. Civilization's ongoing development has modified many of its proclamations. This process is evident even within the Bible itself.

In the Ten Commandments, for example, God claims to visit the sins of the parents upon the third and fourth generation.[8] A few centuries later, the prophet Ezekiel counters that people are held accountable only for their own conduct—not for that of their ancestors.[9]

Other biblical laws were rendered obsolete by history. In Deuteronomy, for example, the Israelites are warned not to return to Egypt.[10] The narrative seems to suggest this is because they were formerly slaves in Egypt, and a supreme effort was required to win their deliverance. Returning to Egypt might mean a return to slavery.

By the time of the Second Temple, however (sixth century BCE to first century CE), this was no longer a concern. There was a continuous flow of people and goods between Judea and Egypt.[11] There was little likelihood that Jews would be re-enslaved en masse. A central reason for the prohibition became moot. It is difficult to believe that God was displeased by this or the people were somehow the worse for it. The law turned out to have only short-term significance. If it was truly eternal, it would not have been overtaken by subsequent events.

8. Exodus 20:5.

9. Ezekiel 18:19.

10. Deuteronomy 17:16 and 28:68.

11. During the fifth century BCE, one Israelite community in Egypt went so far as to build a Temple there, complete with sacrifices, at Elephantine.

## PULLING ONE THREAD

The Bible contains much non-legal narrative as well. Let's consider Joseph of the Book of Genesis and Broadway's *Amazing Technicolor Dreamcoat* fame. From a literary standpoint, the Joseph narrative sets the stage for the story of Egyptian slavery and the freedom that follows. It reaffirms that God maintains a covenantal relationship of protection with his people, the Hebrews. By favoring and shielding Joseph from harm, God preserves the pact he made with his ancestor, Abraham. In addition, the story offers lessons on personal and family life.

Whether the Joseph story comes from a divine or human source should not impact anyone's religious observance. There are no biblically commanded ritual or celebratory mandates in it. If the Joseph saga is a human creation—conceived by storytellers, recorded by scribes, and not given to Moses by God on Mt. Sinai—it should make little difference to a faithful soul.

Except that it does. For if we allow that the Joseph narrative is non-historic, then we must allow that perhaps the Abraham narrative is as well. If that is the case, then the Covenant between God and the Hebrews may be likewise non-historic—at least from God's perspective. We can see why some people are less than eager to pursue this line of inquiry.

But we can go further still. If the Joseph and Abraham narratives are not divinely authored, perhaps the same is true for the story of Moses. If that is the case, it means the entire corpus of biblical law is something other than a God-given revelation.

We see the problem. By pulling on one thread, an entire fabric can unravel. We are not asking these questions for the sake of being provocative. We are asking them in the hope that they might lead us to a deeper understanding of God.

## GOD AND LAW IN THE NARRATIVE

We should stress that even if much of the Bible is neither divinely authored nor "divinely inspired," it does not mean that its narratives, laws, and rituals are without value. But if the Bible is, in fact, a human creation, it does mean that biblical assertions cannot be taken, *ipso facto*, as the final word on any subject. It means that before we accept biblical verses as God's Truth, we need to subject them to the same standards of critical analysis, reason, morality, etc., as we would any other claim.

It also means, at a minimum, that biblical texts by themselves may not be used as a justification to deprive any person of their fundamental human rights, including the right to life and liberty. This is no small point. The belief in Scripture's absolute authority has been responsible for significant discrimination and bloodshed throughout history. It continues today. Much of it might be stopped if we could acknowledge that at least some of those sacred words may be the product of fallible human beings—and not an all-knowing God.

# 7

# Practice and Pursuit

WHILE SEEING THE BIBLE as narrative may call into question any number of religious beliefs and practices, it does not invalidate the legitimacy of religious pursuit. On the contrary, accepting that much of scripture, and the God depicted therein, is the creation of human beings allows us to search with a broader perspective.

It can also liberate us from destructive teachings. The numerous scriptural passages that do not meet our moral standard become easier to set aside.

It also allows us to see ritual in a different light. Many religious leaders lament decreasing numbers of faithful practitioners in their congregations. They are at pains to explain why, in numerous denominations, active participation in ritual and worship is declining. They complain that their co-religionists seek answers to life's great questions outside of the faith rather than within it.

Part of the problem may be that, like the biblical narratives, faith frequently represents rituals created by humans as ordained by God. Many people find this objectionable, often with good reason. When freethinking people's sense of credibility—to say nothing of decency and morality—is offended in the name of what is presented as eternal truth, they will disengage.

§

Many modern religious thinkers have, in fact, worked to re-present sacred texts and practices to align more closely with present-day beliefs and values. In Judaism, the Reform movement has long done exactly this. Newer movements work to do so as well.[1] Conservative and Orthodox Jewish translators of the prayer book are often creative when confronted with what they consider to be problematic passages. There are reformist traditions in Christianity and independent voices in Islam who seek to do the same. Despite this, many denominations—and the congregations that comprise them—do not yet offer a set of belief principles and ritual practices that are current, coherent, and transcendent.

It might help the faithful and the potentially faithful to develop a belief system that can pass the Tragedy Test if religious leaders were more direct in presenting biblical narratives and the principles and practices that derive from them as human-created. Teaching more, "This is what our ancestors believed" and less, "This is God's Eternal Word" can help place faith on firmer intellectual ground.

Within every major faith, there are schools of belief that teach that ancient scripture may have the first word, but it does not necessarily get the last. Rather than repeating "truths" from holy books and forcing them into life situations where they do not fit or apply, we are better off understanding those texts as sacred narratives. They still possess great value—though not necessarily ultimate value.

If we can accept this point about Scripture, it echoes the earlier point we made about God. The keystone message of the biblical narrative is that God rules the world with all-righteous judgment. But just as sacrificing animals is not the only way for us to approach God, neither is this the only way for us to understand God.

---

1. Reconstructionism, Renewal and others.

## PRAYER AND RITUAL

The way we understand God also impacts the way we pray. Traditional prayers, rituals, and religious education typically encourage us to address God as God appears in the biblical narrative, i.e., as personal. Many of them also suggest that God carefully considers our individual requests and needs. If this is a perspective we do not accept, we need to modify our approach.

Religious services in every Western faith contain prayers that ask God to alter the laws of nature or physics on our behalf. Many of them express gratitude to God for having done so in the past. But if God does not really act in such a manner, then these are ultimately "vain prayers," empty and for naught.[2]

Our spiritual lives, formal and informal, might be better served by rituals that present a God who does not operate according to the tenets of ancient folklore. Narratives that describe God as acting in other-worldly or supernatural ways can still be taught, but they should be acknowledged as the legendary understandings they are. They may have important lessons to teach, but they should not be offered as historical or theological reality. Doing so plants the seeds of future disillusion and disaffection.

Despite our strong desire for a supernatural and intervening God who can love us, respond to us individually, and protect us from harm, belief in such a God is not plausible for many. The history of the world, and perhaps our own personal history, argue against the existence of any such Being. If such a God did in fact exist, he would be, as Woody Allen once observed, an under-achiever. Jokes aside, God does not underachieve. God is simply not in the position to achieve anywhere near the number of things that we wish God could.

---

2. Vain prayers are described in Jewish tradition as those that ask God to change what has already been determined. See *Mishnah Berachot* 9:3.

## WHAT WE SAY WHEN WE WORSHIP

Worship is central in every faith community. Among other things, it can tell us what the community believes, or says it believes, about God.

For example, if the prayer book says that God rules the world with justice, favors his chosen servants, protects his loved ones, and answers when we call, this is understood to be the official word. An attentive worshipper whose faith is different, who does not believe that God acts in this way, or perceives that God acts in a different manner altogether, will experience dissonance.

Such dissonance causes many people to push the prayers aside. They may decide not to take them seriously. Or they may simply respond to them out of habit, paying little attention to content. They may focus on other aspects of the worship experience, perhaps the music or the staging, and less on the words that ostensibly define it. They may concentrate on socializing with friends and neighbors, instead of on whatever spiritual potential the worship experience holds.

Others confront the discordant passages head on. There are traditionalists who insist that every word is valid—no matter how elaborate an interpretation is required to sustain it. They may say that what appears untrue on the surface can hold hidden meaning, and it is the worshipper's job to uncover it. And as we've noted, progressive religious movements often edit, rephrase, or remove such passages altogether.

But the purpose of prayer is to draw us closer to God, not to push us further away. We should not have to resort to cognitive dissonance, high-level esoterica, or checking our rational faculties at the sanctuary door in order to make prayer meaningful. Prayer should not be a problematic exercise for those who wish to embrace it at face value.

This is particularly critical for people who visit houses of worship intermittently. If someone is observing a holiday, commemorating a life-cycle event, or spiritually searching, they should not have to leap over cognitive walls in order to create a meaningful religious experience. Non-regulars often analyze those printed and spoken words closely. We can hardly fault them for drawing the conclusions that their plain meaning suggests.

If we are not going to remove every bit of problematic content from the prayer book (which might not be a bad idea) perhaps worship leaders can advise their congregations on the importance of treating some of faith's words more as metaphor and spiritual history, and less as categorical truth.

Worshippers can be taught to respect the various narratives, legends, and stories as representative of earlier strata in the development of their faith. Our ancestors' understanding need not define our relationship with God today.

This may reduce the degree of intellectual and spiritual conflict that some people experience during communal prayer. It can also help us put our personal faith on a more solid foundation.

## SUPERSTITIOUS PRAYERS

We were taught in grade school that superstition owes much of its origin to correlation. For example, walking under a ladder brings bad luck. Of course it does, it's dangerous! Lessons like this convinced me at a young age that superstition was, for all intents and purposes, the province of fools. I resolved to keep as far away from it as possible, and for many years, I did.

At some point, I became aware that a deep vein of superstition runs through Jewish life and culture. There is, for example, the oft-used Yiddish phrase, *keine hora*. It is a reference to the evil eye, and people repeat it in the hope that it will keep bad things from happening to them or their dear ones. Jews say *keine hora* in the face of possible danger and also, interestingly, upon hearing good news. This is ostensibly to prevent fate from following something good with an offsetting calamity.

Because Jewish life was so precarious for so long, the fear that something good would inevitably be followed by something bad worked its way into the collective consciousness. Repeating words in the hope that they will ward off the evil eye may be a baseless superstition, but it can meet a genuine psychological need.

Still, as a youth, I looked at superstition with a mixture of scorn and bemusement. It seemed to be something for people who were confused, perplexed or just plain lost. Clearly, an informed person had to know better.

Be that as it may, when our children arrived I started saying *keine hora* regularly. I don't recall thinking it through but it must have dawned on me that something terrible could happen to our family as easily as not. Moreover, there was little I could do to prevent it. It was an unsettling realization.

We all know that life can be dangerous and random. Catastrophe can find its way to anyone, no matter how seemingly secure or good a person might be. Try as we might, we cannot protect ourselves, much less our children, from the perils abounding in the world. How to cope with such awful knowledge? What can be done about it? Aside from trying to live as rightly as possible, saying *keine hora* may be as good a response as any.

Still, if you asked me if I believed in anything as foolish as an evil eye, I would have dismissed the notion as ridiculous. I continued to look with disdain at the various trinkets, charms, and bracelets that hucksters marketed to keep it away. I had no use for the red string worn by some Ashkenazi Jews or the *hamsa* (hand) used as ornamentation by some Sephardi Jews. When people inquired about such amulets, I would explain that they were superstitious folk customs, nothing more.

Through it all, I kept saying *keine hora*. I knew it was logically inconsistent, but I kept at it anyway. The world *was* random and violent. Accidents and tragedies happened to good people every day. There was plenty to fear, evil eye or no. Saying *keine hora* may have its shortcomings intellectually, but emotionally, it is right on target.

§

Superstitions were criticized by Maimonides and other thinkers as akin to heresy. They reasoned that if there is One God, i.e., One Authority and One Power, then everything that happens, happens because God wills it. They believed that no other force could determine events. Since superstition hinges on the premise that powers besides God somehow hold sway, these philosophers believed that it was self-contradictory for a monotheist to be superstitious.

Maimonides is held in high regard in Jewish life, but he often spoke with two voices—one for the elite and another for the masses. He understood that his high-minded proclamations were more likely to be accepted by the select few than by the multitude.

He was wise in this regard. Superstition remains attractive even for people who say they know better. The possibility of calamity *is* ever-present. So is the need to protect ourselves from it. In this precarious world, we cling to the belief that God is somehow there to shelter and protect us. It is not by chance that the phrase *keine hora* is as well worn as it is.

§

After Tali died, I stopped saying it. At the same time, I have made an effort to remove as much superstitious behavior as possible—including superstitious ritual behavior—from my life. This is not because I have come to appreciate the oneness of God as Maimonides taught it. It is because it became painfully clear that God protects neither me nor my loved ones—nor anyone else, for that matter—from random harm. This is true no matter how many ritual formulas we utter, be they superstitious or prayerful.

The God with whom I will maintain a relationship is not a God who took my daughter because I missed a *keine hora*, or some similar petition, somewhere along the way. To imply that either repeating certain formulas or failing to do so, was somehow connected to our tragedy is completely unacceptable. No God of justice and mercy can act that way.

§

Whatever God there may or may not be, whatever God we may or may not believe in, we can all agree that any God worthy of the name cannot be petty. A God who allows a life to be taken, or not, based on whether we have uttered a certain set of quasi-pious words or not, would be petty beyond belief. Do we really believe that God smites us or our loved ones for such infractions? If this is how God acts, it is tantamount to obscenity. If this is what we believe, it is not much different.

Saying *keine hora* and similar phrases may give us some dissociative comfort, but they are ultimately addressed to a God who is not there. They are props for a faith that will collapse at the worst possible moment and for a God who will fail the Tragedy Test at the worst possible time.

We are better off living without superstition, both of the popular and the sanctioned varieties. Events will take place—or not—of their own accord. They do not happen because an interceding

God orchestrates our affairs in one direction or another. Our personal petitions, be they superstitious or prayerful, have no power to change God's behavior. For the sake of our faith, as well as for our peace of mind, it would be wise to stop believing, and acting, as if they do.

## FAITH—STILL

We see that someone who makes the argument that an all-good and all-powerful personal God rules the world with righteous judgment faces a greater burden of proof than someone who claims that this is not the case.

This is one of the things that makes faith a challenge—particularly for educated people. The ability to think critically puts faith's contradictions front and center. The ready accessibility of alternative belief systems further complicates matters. The correlation between learned individuals and those who identify less strongly with a religious tradition is not as high as it is by chance.

Educated people can—and maybe even should—be believers, too. They need what faith has to offer as much as the next person. But they will be more open to a faith whose teachings cohere with observed reality. They are more likely to embrace a faith that they see as a source of enlightenment and insight as opposed to one of inherently contradictory, unsustainable, or even harmful doctrine.

The domain of faith is not small. Faith can flourish in the human mind as well as in the human imagination. Faith can be found in our aspirations, in our kindness, and in our worthy hopes and dreams.

Faith is alive when we trust. Faith can help us overcome fear. Faith gives us the strength to persevere. Faith speaks in our silences and pulses when we breathe. Faith can motivate us to repair the world and reward us for doing so.

§

Faith can give us the best possible language for all of this. There is no need for us, or our faith, to resort to what is demonstrably not true. There can be a fitting role for the religious imagination in every faith and in every life.

# AN ASIDE TO SPIRITUAL LEADERS—
# AND THOSE WHO LOVE THEM

People often ask rabbis, priests, ministers, imams, and other religious leaders what they consider "ultimate questions." They don't expect us to know every answer, but they do expect us to have studied them seriously.

Spiritual leaders, like the faiths we represent, should not attempt to explain more than we honestly can. When we are faced with a congregant or parishioner in pain, it is better to admit we do not know an answer than to pretend otherwise.

Such an approach gives spiritual leaders the opportunity to demonstrate a combination of intellectual integrity and spiritual humility—rarely a bad thing. Sometimes near-omniscience is projected onto us, and it can be difficult to resist that and all that comes with it. When we acknowledge that we do not have every answer, we teach a lesson that will endure.

Each of us is flawed and limited. So are many of our sacred texts. So is the God we may have once imagined. Our God is not the only one who needs to pass the Tragedy Test. So does our faith, and so do we.

At the same time, spiritual leaders should not misrepresent religious imagination as religious fact. If we expect people to live with faith, the distinction should be clear. Myths and legends can be taught with an eye towards the lessons they hold, but faith must not pretend to know what it does not. It has enough to offer without resorting to that.

If the teachings of religious and spiritual traditions were all they are sometimes claimed to be, those of us who engage with them earnestly would have by this time solved life's greatest mysteries. We have not. Mythology aside, neither did the great sages of the past. While the human race has grown tremendously in knowledge over the millennia, we do not yet understand why—or even if there is a why—the innocent suffer.

Our sacred texts are the sum total of our as yet unsuccessful attempts to comprehend some of the more complex whys of the universe. Those texts remain more than worthy of our time. Even if they cannot lay claim to perfection, they can lay the foundation for a consecrated life.

We are more likely to grow in our faith if we acknowledge that no matter how grounding and inspiring it may be, it too will reach a point that says, "I do not know." That may be frustrating or disappointing, but it is also honest. Faith at its best embraces honesty. It is also an excellent point from which to go forward.

# 8

# Offering Comfort

## WORDS THAT HEAL, WORDS THAT HARM

MOST OF US RECOGNIZE how important it is to offer comfort in the wake of loss. We all want to help our friends and loved ones, but we may not have the knowledge, or the skills, we need. The right words are not easy to find—and the wrong ones are. Many of the wrong ones come from misapplied religious narratives.

## EVERYTHING WORKS OUT IN THE END

Sometimes people attempt to offer comfort with the phrase, "Everything will work out in the end." They do it with the best of intentions, but it can be a terrible thing to say.

We were told late on the night of Talia's accident that while she remained technically alive, there was no real chance she would survive. Arriving at the airport early the next morning, I informed the check-in agent that we were dealing with a medical emergency and asked if there was anything she could do to help smooth our journey. Specifically, I asked for seats near the front of the plane, so we could exit and be on our way to the hospital as quickly as possible. Privacy would have been a bonus. As luck would have it, the flight was not full. With compassion and professionalism, she moved us forward, to a row by ourselves. It was exactly what we needed.

What we did not need was her going on to tell us how she was sure that "everything would work out in the end." Her intent, no doubt, was to be reassuring, but it had the opposite effect. I thanked her for her caring but could not help but reply that I was afraid it didn't look as though it would.

Leaving the airport in Washington, we took a taxi. When we asked the driver to take us to the hospital, he sensed our distress and asked why we were going. In no mood for conversation but not wanting to be rude, I outlined the circumstances. He listened carefully—and then told us he was sure that everything would work out in the end.

Unlike the airline agent, the driver exhibited numerous signs of religious faith, with markers on his person and in his cab. He expounded that "God is merciful and will certainly save your wonderful daughter." Again, at that point we were quite sure this was not going to be the case. His insistence that things would end happily only made matters worse.

We were traumatized to begin with and intimated for him to stop—to no avail. He went so far as to give us his card—telling us to call him "when, not if, but when," our daughter recovered. Of course that call was never made.

I bear no ill will towards either the airline agent or taxi driver. It is natural for caring people to try to offer reassurance. Most of the time it is welcome. Perhaps most of the time things do work out in the end.

But this time, the words were of no comfort at all. Words of encouragement or acceptance are one thing. Under the circumstances, these were words of denial.

There are certainly times when things do work out. Someone loses a job and, though it seems calamitous at the moment, a new opportunity arises. Greater fulfillment and success come in the new position than would have been possible in the old one. Everything worked out in the end.

But it doesn't always. Perhaps along with the job, the family lost its health insurance. This time, no suitable replacement employment could be found. This time, a member of the family contracted a serious illness. Without insurance, college and retirement savings were depleted, the house foreclosed, and the credit rating ruined. For lack of affordable treatment, the illness became life-threatening. The stress eventually destroyed the marriage. Under such circumstances, "Everything will work out in the end," might have been the worst possible words to offer.

We'll pray for you. We'll keep a good thought for you. Even, May God be with you. These can be better choices in a crisis than, "Everything will work out in the end." Sometimes it doesn't.

## GOD DOESN'T GIVE PEOPLE ANY MORE THAN THEY CAN HANDLE

We may have also heard people say, "God doesn't give people any more than they can handle." Interestingly, the closest scriptural equivalent comes not from the Bible but the *Qur'an*.[1]

We may know people who managed to find strength from within to overcome a great crisis. We may also know people—of great faith, of little faith or of no faith—who were burdened by far more than they could handle. Drug addiction, depression, PTSD, suicide, and more provide ample testimony.

There are at least two potential problems in telling someone that God doesn't give people more than they can handle. The first is that we can never know anyone else's breaking point. The second is that it portrays God as inflicting the suffering.

There are other ways to understand God. And better words to offer.

1. *Qur'an* 2:286, "On no soul doth Allah place a burden greater than it can bear."

## KARMA AND SUCH

Whenever someone seems to be on the short end of fate's stick, we often hear the uncharitable sentiment, "What goes around comes around," or simply, *karma*. *Karma* is an ancient Hindu principle, but there are parallel teachings in many faiths and cultures, both religious and secular.

Rabbi Hillel the Elder offered a first-century Jewish version of the doctrine. Upon seeing a skull floating on the water he is reported to have said, "Because you drowned others, you were drowned; and those who drowned you will themselves be drowned."[2]

We also find the credo in Christianity and Islam. The New Testament reads, "For in the same way you judge others, you will be judged, and with the measure you use, it will be measured to you."[3] The *Qur'an* says, "And whoever does a speck of good [in life], will see it [on the Day of Judgment]. And whoever does a speck of evil, will see it."[4] The title of Shakespeare's play *Measure for Measure* evokes the same premise.[5]

Whenever people flout the rules of law or decency and appear to get away with it, it troubles us. In the face of such behavior, belief in *karma*, by whatever name, reassures us. It affirms that however things may appear at the moment, God will get the final word—and that word will be just.

§

But since faith in the one Just God first evolved, inquisitive children, skeptical adolescents, and mature adults alike have questioned the principle. We have no proof that *karma* is real. The fact that dots appear connected from time to time does not a law of the

---

2. *Mishnah Avot* 2:6. This is an expression of the Rabbinic belief that divine justice follows the principle of "*middah k'neged middah*—measure for measure." See *Mishnah Sotah* 1:7.

3. Matthew 7:2.

4. *Qur'an* 100:7–8.

5. The play also raises the question of whether "measure for measure" is true justice or not.

universe make. Especially when we take into consideration how often the dots don't seem to be connected at all.

Do the families of the millions who died as a result of Hitler's crimes take any real comfort in the abstract possibility that he may be burning in hell? Or that he may have been reincarnated as some lower life form?[6] No matter how much he may be suffering in the next world (and of course we have no evidence that he is), it cannot come close to atoning for the crimes he committed or the horror he caused. *Karma*? Balance? Justice? Don't we wish.

6. Reincarnation is another doctrine based on the belief that God is ultimately, perfectly just.

## SHE IS WITH GOD

Charlie Brown: "Admission to Heaven is graded on a curve."
Linus: "How do you know?"
Charlie Brown: "I'm always sure about things
that are a matter of opinion."[7]

"She is in a higher place, a better place."
"She was too good for this world."
"Her work here was done."
"God needed her in heaven and took her to be with him."
We heard each of these phrases, and others like them, after Tali died. They were offered with sincerity and caring. All were expressions of faith in an afterlife, a place-time in which God lovingly rectifies all the injustices of this world.

We don't know whether or not any of these are true, but we understand why people say them. Earthly injustice is only coherent in the cosmic scheme of things if there is a life after this one in which the good are rewarded, and the wrong is set right.

The comfort people receive from this belief explains why, since time immemorial, humanity has told as many versions of the afterlife narrative as it has. Most of them attempt to solve the problem of how a just God can allow otherwise unjustifiable suffering. If there is genuine justice in the next world, the injustices in this one become at least somewhat easier to accept. If you believe in an afterlife, you, your faith, and your God will have a much easier time passing the Tragedy Test.

If you are such a believer, or care to be one, may your belief give you strength.

If we are not, or are not sure, our response to tragedy needs to somehow come from the only world we know for certain.

7. Schultz, *Beagles and Bunnies*, 32.

## BECAUSE GOD LOVES YOU

There is a Talmudic doctrine known as "chastisements of love" and it, too, is sometimes offered to victims of a tragedy. It states that the righteous are being punished because God loves them.[8]

Yes, you read that right. God brings suffering and death to the good among us because he loves us, and this, in some inscrutable way, is good for us. If that sounds like something between abusive and perverse to you, rest assured you are not alone. A God who acts in such a way would be far more malevolent than Shalom Auslander's "punk."

Not everyone accepted this idea, even when it first appeared during the early centuries of the Common Era. In the words of one sage, "I desire neither the chastisements nor their reward!"[9]

Few people today will accept the notion that calamitous personal suffering is an act of love intentionally visited upon us by a benevolent God. For most of us, a God who punishes good people, whether out of declared love or unfathomable mystery, is a God unworthy of our devotion.

We are loath to accept such behavior in parents, spouses, friends, or neighbors. Why should we accept it from the Highest we can know? We have been taught that the way of God is to do righteousness and justice.[10] If that is true, it is difficult to see where so-called punishments of love fit in.

If a doctrine like this is what it takes to believe in a God who is acting with purpose and intention, it may be time to find another understanding.

---

8. *Babylonian Talmud, Berachot* 5a; There are parallels here to the New Testament's description of the Passion. My comments here should be taken from a Jewish perspective only.

9. *Babylonian Talmud, Berachot* 5b.

10. Genesis 18:19.

# GOD IS WEEPING

People in grief are sometimes told that God is weeping along with them. This idea is found in both classical and modern Jewish and Christian thought.

It is a way of saying that God is not responsible for our sorrow, but that our sorrow is real and it has moved God's own self to cry. It does seem to comfort some people.

It is a model, however, that portrays God as helpless in the face of tragedy and injustice. It gives us a weak personal God who is defeated by forces greater than himself.

It may work for some people, but it doesn't work for me. I need strength from my God, not weakness—and certainly not helplessness. I already have people to weep with. Most survivors of tragedy do not need additional tears; we have enough of our own.

I know that it is all right to cry. I do not need God to tell me this. I need God to help lift me up.

# 9

# Luck Happens

IN ONE WAY OR another, all of the aforementioned words of offered comfort are expressions of the belief that there was a reason for—and a purpose behind—the tragedy. They insinuate, intentionally or not, that God had it in for the victim—for God's own good reasons. They also, wittingly or not, cast the speaker as knowing God's mind. This is something that no non-prophet should pretend to know.

We are aware that material blessing and success can be a function of hard work, good fortune, or both. And that tragedy and ill fortune can be the result of a personal shortcoming or character deficiency. But we cannot discount the role of luck. The lives our parents lead do more to determine the course of our own lives than any other factor—and none of us chooses our parents.

Everything from health to wealth to life itself can be won or lost through luck. This is not to say that we should give less than our all to everything we do. But even when we make our sincerest efforts, there is no guarantee that chance won't determine the outcome.

It may be comforting to believe that some benevolent and purposeful master plan exists, and that whatever happens was "meant to be." But in our world, the belief that righteousness is faithfully rewarded and wickedness reliably punished is continually found wanting. It may be true every now and then—but most of us want more consistency from our faith than that.

Whenever people have tried to make order out of the world's chaos, poets, charlatans, philosophers, and holy men have arisen to offer answers. But if there truly is a higher plan, it remains beyond our ability to fathom. Take this illustration from a baseball fan.

§

In the fall of 2006, the New York Mets were playing the St. Louis Cardinals for the pennant—the championship of the National League. The teams were tied at three games apiece, and the winner of the seventh game would go to the World Series.

With the score 1-1 in the top of the sixth inning and one man on base, Cardinal slugger Scott Rolen hit a ball to deep left field. Running back to the ball, and the wall, outfielder Endy Chavez leaped high and made a catch that could only be described as sensational—reaching over the fence and robbing Rolen of a sure home run. For good measure, he fired the ball back to the infield in time to catch the runner off base for a double play.

It was an effort that took away the breath of Mets fans, and baseball fans, everywhere. Television announcer Joe Buck asked, "Have we ever seen better?" Few could say that they had. Surely, believers in baseball gods everywhere had their sign. The Mets were going to win the pennant. After a play like that, it was clearly "meant to be."

Except that it wasn't. A two-run Cardinal home run in the top of the ninth inning broke the tie and put St. Louis ahead. With two outs in the bottom of the ninth and the winning run on base, the Mets' star outfielder Carlos Beltran looked at a called third strike to end the game. It wasn't meant to be after all.

After the contest, veteran Cardinal manager Tony LaRussa was asked whether he thought "Endy's catch" was a sign from on high that his team was going to lose. He dismissed the notion with a chuckle. "Oh no," he said. "There's no script in baseball."

Indeed, there isn't. It is one of the reasons we keep watching it—and all other sports, for that matter. We never know how the game is going to turn out. Sometimes our guys win, sometimes the other team does. But either way, as everyone who has watched their share of sports knows, LaRussa is right—there is no script.

Sports fans may appreciate better than most the words of Ecclesiastes, "The race is not necessarily to the swift nor the battle to the strong . . . but time and chance happen to them all."[1]

Of course, Ecclesiastes was talking about more serious matters than ballgames. But if time and chance determine athletic contests—which are among the most rule-bound and regulated of all human activities—how much greater must their influence be in everyday life, where the variables are infinitely greater?

1. Ecclesiastes 9:11.

## LUCK AND GOD

*Mazal tov* is a familiar Jewish expression. It is used to wish someone congratulations or, more literally, good luck. There are parallel phrases in most cultures. You can find people wishing one another safety from random and hostile forces pretty much everywhere on earth.

Once upon a time though, *mazal tov* had a different connotation. The original meaning of the word *mazal* was "planet" or "constellation." *Tov,* then as now, means "good." So when you said *mazal tov* you were actually wishing someone a "good planet" or "good constellation," i.e., that their stars and planets would align favorably.

We see that at least some Jewish belief was once more closely tied to astrology. In ages past, Jews—and most others—studied the night skies intently. They believed the stars and planets hinted at what God, or the gods, were up to.[2]

For most of us, astrology is junk science, if that. But even if we do not accept that the stars and planets play a role in determining the course of our lives, we know that any number of things beyond our control affect us profoundly. Instead of stars and planets, we moderns attribute what otherwise seems inexplicable to luck, fortune, or fate.

It can be disturbing to admit this. If luck is real, it means that we are in less than full command of our destiny. It means that greater forces can and do get in the way of our hopes and dreams, no matter how noble they might be. It also means that luck can foil the loving, caring and protecting powers of the just God we all wish were supreme.

§

We do everything we can to minimize the influence of luck, certainly of bad luck. We work to build our lives on earned merit. We avoid taking unnecessary risks. We buy insurance. All of this

2. Archeologists have in fact uncovered depictions of the zodiac in the ruins of ancient synagogues.

helps—but only to a point. There will always be matters and circumstances that are beyond our control. We will always need luck.

The reality of luck also renders belief in an all-powerful and all-just God problematic. It is why wishing or claiming luck, either good or bad, is discouraged by some of the stricter monotheists. To little avail. People always find a way to wish one another good luck, whatever their nominal faith may have to say on the subject.

Luck can explain good fortune or bad, oft times more coherently than belief in a just God. It can account for why things go wrong and for why there is unwarranted suffering. It explains why *karma* seems to work only sometimes.

It appears more rational to accept that luck has an outsize effect on our lives than to insist that everything happens for a reason, that everything is meant to be, or that everything that happens is an expression of God's will. Luck offers testimony that God's reach is limited.

But luck also allows us to say that God does not intend for the forces of nature to harm the innocent. Luck explains why cancer, earthquakes, and air force bombs kill good people as well as bad. Luck allows us to understand that things can and do happen, metaphysically speaking, for no reason at all.

§

Ecclesiastes is not alone in his observation that time and chance, perhaps even more than God's inscrutable will, determine outcomes. There is a word for the unpredictable in every language. It tells us—whether we want to admit it or not—that in life, as in sports, there is no script.

Or, more precisely, sooner or later the unscripted appears. When it does, it can be either life-saving or life-destroying. What are the effects of disease, accident, hurricane, tidal wave, earthquake, financial turmoil, family crisis, betrayal of trust, street crime, terror, acts of war, "acts of God," if not manifestations of time and chance? Ecclesiastes was correct; they happen to us all.

And we are left to ponder. Was it meant to be? Did it happen for a reason? Was it *karma?* Was God giving us what he thought we could handle? Will everything work out in the end? There are times when we may be able to look back and say yes.

But often we cannot. When the stakes are high, especially if a beloved human life is the price, the same belief means that God has chosen to rip a hole in our hearts for no intelligible reason.

Is this the God we want to believe in? Is this the God we want to serve? Is this who God really is?

## TRUTH AND JUSTICE

"We who are faithful may not ignore
that which human intelligence proves.
We may not lie to ourselves and call that which is false, true
nor that which is true, false."[3]
—RABBI MORDECHAI BREUER

Every faith teaches that God is Truth. It is not always easy to accept truth where we find it, but there comes a point when both our faith and our integrity demand it.

From time to time, we may claim to see the hand of God, fate or *karma* working in our lives. What we are more likely witnessing are the effects of the laws of physics and nature.

We can ascribe whatever intent we wish to those laws, but scientifically speaking, events happen because it is determined that they will. The laws of physics and nature, along with the free will we exercise within their parameters, lie behind what we may think of as fate or destiny. They create outcomes that can be either moral, immoral, or amoral.

When being given a serious or terminal diagnosis, people commonly ask their doctors, "Why?" Unless lifestyle factors are an obvious culprit (and sometimes even when they are), physicians typically answer with references to bad luck, mystery, ignorance, or some combination of the three. These are honest responses because most often, we don't really know.

§

At the same time, we learn that while we attempt to exercise as much control over our personal fate as possible, we eventually come to realize that fate has far more control over us than the other way around.

3. Breuer (1921–2007) was an Orthodox Israeli rabbi who developed what he called *shitat habechinot*—the dual aspect approach; i.e., one that incorporates both traditional and modern-critical understandings of the Hebrew Bible.

Beyond the control of all of us is death. Few of us want to die. No one wants a loved one to die young. When we lose someone we never expected to lose, someone we would have given absolutely anything—up to and including our own lives to save—we cannot help but recognize how little control we have over that which is most important to us.

Luck. Mystery. Our own ignorance. We will not understand much about life until and unless we give them their due.

§

All of this means that it takes considerable mental jujitsu to insist that God remains the proactive arbiter of our lives. It also requires a willingness to disregard portions of the Bible itself.

The Hebrews were enslaved for four hundred years before God heard their cries and freed them. If "justice delayed is justice denied,"[4] then even that prototypical liberation points to a God who is something less than entirely just.

The generations-long delay before they were freed made whatever justice that ensued meaningless for those who saw no hint of it while they lived, slaved, and died. Only those who took part in the actual exodus got to appreciate that their suffering may have been for some higher purpose. From then until now, countless numbers of God's children have suffered randomly, cruelly, and unremittingly for no discernible purpose.

It should not be difficult to reject the belief that such suffering is somehow good for us, even if a measure of good eventually comes from it. Yes, it is true that working through agony can make us more empathetic. Among other things, it can motivate us to work to make the world a kinder and gentler place. But none of this remotely offsets the pain we endure along the way. Besides, there are less agonizing ways to learn these lessons and incorporate their values into our lives.

A colleague once tried to counsel me on this. He pointed out that the experience of losing a child helped make me more feeling,

4. After *Mishnah, Avot* 5:7.

a better listener, more understanding, etc. "Maybe," I told him. "But it was still a horrible trade."

It seems clear that the earthly justice humanity receives from the "true, perfect and righteous judge" is neither all-just nor all-perfect—to say nothing of all-merciful. The truth is, in fact, often irredeemably horrible.

Fortunately, there are other ways to understand God, and we turn to them now.

# Part II—RESPONSE

# 10

# The God of Law and Spirit

"I Will Be What I Will Be"[1]
—EXODUS 3:14

LEST WE TAKE LIFE's blessings for granted, all of the great religions teach their adherents to express gratitude to God regularly. When good things happen, people of faith will offer one variation or another on the words, "Thank God." Many nominally secular people do so as well.

At the same time, we are counseled to offer sacred words when bad things happen. Upon hearing news of a death, observant Jews will say "Blessed is the True Judge." Christians might offer that their loved one has been "called home." Islam teaches that nothing happens, good or bad, that is not intended by God. Eastern religions speak of *karma*'s wheel.

---

1. God's Name—אהיה אשר אהיה, communicated to Moses by God at the burning bush in the wilderness.

Inasmuch as loss is inevitable in human life, every faith also offers guides for maintaining equanimity in the face of it. With a combination of understanding and resilience, we can recover—at least partially and maybe significantly. Maintaining a connection to God in times of loss—even to a God we do not understand, even to a God we may feel has let us down—can give us strength. Ultimately, we all need to go on.

## UNDERSTANDING GOD:
## GROWING AS WE DO

Karen Armstrong is an Oxford scholar and author. She has suggested that one of her books, *A History of God*, may have prompted a reviewer's observation that for many in the modern world, Friedrich Nietzsche was right: God is dead. This is not to say that God is really dead, but rather our ideas of God have not evolved along with our understanding of human history. Our view of God has not kept pace with the complex questions that the modern world has forced upon us.[2]

In other words, our views of God do not necessarily develop along with the rest of us. We often cling to the God-ideas we were taught as children, no matter how great the disconnect between them and our subsequent life experiences. But unless we intend to go through life tethered to a God who is functionally "dead," it is best if our understanding of the divine matures along with the rest of us.

For anyone weaned on the idea of a personal God—and that includes most everyone with roots in the Judeo-Christian tradition—this is no small step. We prefer that our personal relationships be, well, personal—warm, close, and comforting, whether we are relating to one another or to the "Almighty." But our relationships with one another and our relationship with God cannot be the same. God is simply too great.

We have already examined the possibility that God is not personal. If God is not personal and does not intervene to save us from undeserved suffering, then what exactly is God? No one has yet answered this question fully, and we will not be the first. But we may be able to answer it partially.

2. Personal communication to the author.

## REASON AND METAPHYSICS

Once again, I understand the physics that caused my daughter's death. They are not complicated. When a jogger is struck by a large vehicle motoring at speed, there is little doubt what the outcome will be. But what of the metaphysics? What higher meaning, if any, was there in this tragedy? As we have seen, the categories of possibility are fairly limited.

There were periods in my life when any number of the explanations we have examined might have been satisfactory—either in whole, in part, or in combination. Academically, intellectually, or around the seminar table, a case can be made for each. But faith is not meant to be lived in a classroom, it is intended to apply to life in all of its fullness. The rationales no longer work for me—neither in my head nor in my heart. And I am enough of a pastor to understand that no one can insist that they must.

So this leads to the possibility that Tali died for no higher, divinely ordained reason at all. That she did not die to teach anyone a lesson—though we have learned much since. That she was not killed to punish either her or us—though we are profoundly wounded. That she was not killed because God wanted to show his love for her—that is simply wretched. That she did not die that others might live—even though that has in fact been the case. That she did not die in order to help us grow—although we certainly have.

It is possible to believe that her death was not orchestrated by a loving God to bring about *any* particular outcome. It is possible that Tali died for no metaphysical reason at all.

## GOD PLAYS BY THE RULES

"The rain fell alike upon the Just and the Unjust,
and for nothing was there a why and a wherefore."[3]
—W. Somerset Maugham

If this is so, then where is God in our tragedy? The answer may be simple. If God established and determined the laws of physics and nature, and operates within those laws, Talia was a casualty of them. *Fini.*

This conclusion gives us an answer to the question "Why?" that is both comprehensible and reasonable: her death was an accident. In our world and in our universe, accidents happen. They happen for no reason other than the laws of physics and nature determine that they do. As the ancient Rabbis acknowledged, "the world is governed by its rules."[4] There is no more mystery than that.

This conclusion may be stark and even painful, but accepting it can help us pass the Tragedy Test. At the same time, accepting it need not mark the end of our faith. It can mark the point where we encounter the God of Law and Spirit.

3. Maugham, *Of Human Bondage,* 558.
4. *Babylonian Talmud, Avodah Zarah* 54b.

## THE GOD OF LAW AND SPIRIT

Neither Moses Maimonides in the twelfth century, nor Albert Einstein in the twentieth, believed in a personal God. As we have seen, Maimonides taught that the God who is caring and loving—i.e., personal and intervening—is better understood as a necessary belief than an existential reality. Because he believed that God was a perfect unity, any action or movement that God might take to intervene in the affairs of humanity would, *ipso facto*, violate that unity.

Maimonides' medieval view keeps distinguished modern company. Knowledgeable as he was about the workings of the universe, Einstein was often asked for his thoughts on God and religion. He was not hesitant to offer them.

> " . . . I do not believe in the God of theology who rewards good and punishes evil. My God created laws that take care of that. His universe is not ruled by wishful thinking, but by immutable laws."

> " . . . I believe in [Benedict] Spinoza's God, who reveals himself in the lawful harmony of the world, not in a God who concerns himself with the fate and the doings of mankind."[5]

> " . . . Nobody, certainly, will deny that the idea of the existence of an omnipotent, just, and omni-beneficent personal God is able to accord man solace, help, and guidance; also, by virtue of its simplicity, it is accessible to the most undeveloped mind. But, on the other hand, there are decisive weaknesses attached to this idea in itself, which have been painfully felt since the beginning of history."[6]

While he is held in higher regard as a physicist than as a theologian, Einstein's statement that humanity leans towards personal,

---

5. Spinoza, a seventeenth-century Dutch Jewish philosopher, espoused the idea that God and nature were two names for the same reality.

6. Cline, *Denying*, para. 2, 8, 11.

anthropomorphic characterizations of God because they make God more accessible, is insightful.

It is challenging for us to rise above such characterizations. But if we wish to come to terms with what has been, as he puts it, painfully felt since the beginning of history, e.g., the unjust suffering of the innocent and the righteous, we should make the effort to do so.[7]

Because they counter the plain sense of most biblical narratives, non-personal conceptions of God are less widely embraced than more traditional ones. But accepting God as non-personal has the enormous advantage of allowing us to resolve that God is not some kind of cosmic puppet-master who orchestrates our sorrows.

It enables us to accept that there may not be any transphysical reason or higher meaning behind a given catastrophe. It gives us a God who is consistent with the laws of nature. It gives us a God who does not contradict the prototypical divine attributes of justice and mercy. It gives us a God who allows us to believe that terrible accidents can simply happen.

At the same time, the spirit of this non-personal God can be found in acts of goodness, wisdom, truth, compassion, love, and justice. In other words, in the virtues and qualities that every religious tradition identifies with the divine. This spirit is alive within people and perhaps even within nature itself.

I refer to this non-personal God as the God of Law and Spirit.

7. Einstein expanded on his comments about Spinoza's and his own ideas on religion in response to a question from New York's Rabbi Herbert Goldstein in 1929: "I can understand your aversion to the use of the term 'religion' to describe an emotional and psychological attitude which shows itself most clearly in Spinoza . . . I have not found a better expression than 'religious' for the trust in the rational nature of reality that is, at least to a certain extent, accessible to human reason."—see Cline, *Religion and Science*, para. 5.

## ALTHOUGH THIS GOD CAN'T ACCOUNT FOR EVERYTHING, EITHER

Like the God of most religious traditions, the God of Law and Spirit may not give us what we consider a satisfactory answer to every question. But this is, in part, because understanding God as congruous with the laws of nature renders certain questions meaningless.

For example, if someone were to ask, "How can 2+2=5?" we would immediately dismiss the question as irrational and ridiculous. Anything other than 2+2=4 violates the laws of mathematics. The only way 2+2 can equal 5 is if we somehow transform the value of 2, +, =, or 5. This is clearly something we cannot do, at least not within our present space-time configuration.

Similarly, this is why there are no real answers to questions like, "How could God take my daughter's life?" Such questions only make sense if God could somehow alter the laws of nature in order to take a given action. It is not possible for the God of Law and Spirit to do this—any more than it is possible for us to add 2+2 and have it equal 5. The question is ultimately absurd.

People have been asking why tragedies happen since before the belief in an all-powerful, all-just and all-merciful God arose. But if God is indeed the non-personal God of Law and Spirit, it allows us to conclude:

- that the laws of physics and nature are determinative and all-encompassing.

- that these laws can create tragic outcomes—for no higher purpose or reason.

- that God does not actively intervene to prevent undeserved suffering or human evil.

- that God nevertheless lives in the spirits of goodness, wisdom, compassion, love, and justice that are around us and within us.

And that God's power to see that goodness prevails, is limited.

## GOD'S POWER IS LIMITED

Goodness, wisdom, compassion, love, and justice may be Godly qualities, but they do not always carry the day.

This is an understanding that can help us be more accepting of loss. Whatever comfort comes from it may not be as soothing as we would like, but we don't need to reimagine the laws of the universe in order to receive it. At the same time, understanding God as Law and Spirit does not require us to offer answers for which there is no evidence.

Those who attempt to live their lives in harmony with the God of Law and Spirit are not assured that they will be richly rewarded or spared harm. Recognizing Law, their faith will cohere with the standards of reason and the laws of nature—come what may. At the same time, if they are in service to Spirit, they will be regarded as pursuers of integrity and kindness.

This may not be all the comfort that we want, but insofar as it goes, it will endure.

## THE GOD OF LAW AND SPIRIT
## —AND TRAGEDY

If we are correct in our understanding of the God who is Law and Spirit, it means that God does not willfully perpetrate disasters. Nor are disasters a means by which God demonstrates power or judgment. They are, instead, a consequence of the laws of the universe.

When these laws bring about what we consider an unfair or unjust outcome, we call it a tragedy. Likewise, when we engage in careless or evil conduct, calamity may ensue. Violent human behavior can take on a life of its own and bring about further misfortune. As the Rabbis taught, "When the forces of destruction are unleashed, they do not distinguish between righteous and wicked."[8] They were not referring to meteorites, volcanoes or tidal waves. They were referring to the havoc caused when human beings act contrary to the divine spirit of justice and love.

The God of Law and Spirit does not pass the Tragedy Test by giving us heartening metaphysical reasons or explanations for our losses. Instead, this God gives us the understanding that tragedies happen because forces of destruction are continually being let loose in the universe—by nature and human beings alike. Those forces cause pain, suffering, and death—justly and not. All too often, the spirits of justice, love, wisdom, and caring are overpowered by nature's immutable laws. More's the pity, but this is our reality.

It is always tempting to believe that the universe functions on some higher moral plane, but we may better understand this as wishful thinking. Wishful thinking can be powerful and even healing. It can tell us that our loved ones are with God—safe and happy in heaven. It can tell us that God took them because God needed them, or because their work on earth was done. It can tell us that God weeps along with us. It can tell us that for our own betterment, God told us, "No."

8. *Babylonian Talmud, Bava Kama* 60a.

We offer such words to one another when we are desperate for reassurance. We may one day realize they were born of that spirit, and that can cause us further pain.

If we want our faith to pass the Tragedy Test, it may be better to look for whatever comfort there is to be had where the truth is more demonstrable and less precarious.

## THE GOD OF LAW AND SPIRIT—
## ALIVE IN ALL OF US

Saying that God is found in the laws of nature is not meant to suggest that God is small. Nature's laws consist of more than cause and effect and the survival of the fittest. The laws of nature rule the heavens, the earth, and all that is in them. They can be found in the human heart as well.

We can sense the God of Law and Spirit when we do good deeds. We can experience the God of Law and Spirit when we further the cause of justice. We can feel the God of Law and Spirit where there is healing. We can touch the God of Law and Spirit when we embrace artistic and musical beauty. We can grow with the God of Law and Spirit when we nurture our spirituality.

We can live with the God of Law and Spirit when we join others in seeking a higher life path. We can find the God of Law and Spirit when we make peace. We can touch the God of Law and Spirit where there is love. We can discover the God of Law and Spirit as we attempt to recover from loss.

# GOD IS ONE—UNDERSTANDINGS ARE MANY

Despite this understanding, some of us may wish to continue a relationship with a God we think of as personal. Our personal God can seem strong, close, and real in ways that the God of Law and Spirit may not.

Even if the personal God cannot pass the Tragedy Test without resorting to leaps of religious or metaphysical imagination, faith in such a God can strengthen us nonetheless. For those who wish to maintain such a relationship, I am not here to take it away. And it may be possible to maintain a relationship with a personal God and the God of Law and Spirit simultaneously.

F. Scott Fitzgerald wrote that the test of a first-rate intelligence is the ability to hold two opposed ideas in mind at the same time and retain the ability to function.[9] If our relationship with God is going to be functional, and we are up to the challenge, we may be able to hold onto both perceptions.

We can take what we need from each, calling upon them at different times for different needs. This does not mean that there are two Gods. It means that our understanding of God is multifaceted. At least one of those facets can help get us through tragedy. Together they can help get us through life.

9. Fitzgerald, *The Crack-Up,* 69.

# 11

# Reason—A Gift from God

WE MODERNS GENERALLY DO not like being told that something is inexplicable. We have a thirst for understanding, and it is a disposition that has served us well. We have looked for, and found, scientific explanations for innumerable phenomena previously thought of as incomprehensible. In the process, we've extended the boundaries of physics, technology, medicine, engineering, and more.

Our ancient ancestors may not have possessed our knowledge or tools, but they sought understanding no less than we do—and they were willing to push boundaries in order to get it. Even the nominal monotheists among them would, from time to time, say that otherwise unfathomable events were the workings of angels and demons.[1]

Angels and demons are the products of our imagination. They do not exist in real life. People rely on them to explain how a world that is supposed to be under the authority of a just and benevolent God often appears not to be.

But such a world can also be explained by a God who does not orchestrate every phenomenon under the sun. It can be explained by a God who is not the all-enforcing God of justice.

1. Mostly demons. People are rarely driven to spiritual distraction by good fortune.

Saying that the disorder and injustice around us are an inscrutable mystery is something of an evasion. We can solve the riddle easily enough. We just need to be willing to accept solutions that point to a non-personal God whose powers are more limited than we wish they were.

At some point, it becomes a matter of faith. I suggest we embrace a faith that is not contradicted by reason. A faith that, insofar as it goes, will not mislead or betray us. A faith that allows us to find comfort from sources we can trust.

## QUESTIONS FROM THE COSMOS

Sometime between three and four billion years from now, scientists estimate that the star that is our sun will burn through its supply of hydrogen fuel and begin to self-destruct. At some point during this process, all life on Earth will come to an end. While at the moment there are more pressing issues, these facts raise some significant questions for believers. Did God intend for it to happen? If so, why? If not, who, if anyone, did?

The ancients did not know that the sun and the earth would one day die from natural causes. Had they known, some of their faith principles might have evolved differently. Would they have still believed that God was benevolent, loving and kind? Could they have reconciled the planet's future destruction with the fact that it will have nothing whatsoever to do with humankind's behavior? Would they have wondered what kind of designer implants a self-destruct device in his most glorious creation? Might it have made them less certain that God was the omnipotent creator?

Modern science also reckons with near certainty that there is intelligent life on distant worlds. This knowledge raises questions about the Bible's creation narrative and on God's connection to humanity. It challenges the notion that we are the only ones in the universe with whom God has a relationship.

A living faith is stronger when it accounts for scientific fact, in addition to traditional legend. Philosopher Benedict Spinoza in the seventeenth century and American rabbi Mordecai Kaplan in the twentieth are two among many who sought to reconcile them. Spinoza concluded that God was one with nature and its laws. Kaplan understood God "as the power that makes for salvation."[2] We could say that Spinoza recognized God as Law, while Kaplan understood God as Spirit.

2. Kaplan, *Meaning of God*, 40.

Each derived his insight from the God of the Bible, but each saw God as different from the God of religious traditions. A full treatment of the ideas of these scholars can be found elsewhere. For us, it is sufficient to say that if we are going to recognize modern scientific truths, our faith needs a place for understandings of God that acknowledge them as well.

## SCRIPTURE AND SCIENCE

While most people today place considerable trust in science, science once taught that the sun revolved around the earth. Science once made no connection between the eastern continental outline of South America and the western shoreline of Africa—or, for that matter, between smoking and cancer. As recently as the mid-twentieth century, psychiatrists were prescribing frontal lobotomies for patients with conditions ranging from schizophrenia to depression to anxiety. Given this track record, we might be tempted to do away with science altogether. The reason we don't is that science has a record of learning from its mistakes.

Faith, like science, has promulgated its own share of erroneous notions. The idea that God, or the gods, desired human sacrifice, sacred prostitution, and wholesale murder are example enough. But faith, too, has learned from its mistakes.

It may be that science learns more quickly. But just as we don't abandon science for its failings, neither should we abandon faith for its. Science speaks haltingly, if at all, on the indispensable subjects of love, caring, devotion, ethics, service, and holiness. Faith is fluent in all of these. But science and scholarship can provide us with essential insight when it comes to the subject of faith.

## WHAT GOD IS NOT

Science and scholarship make it clear that the world is far older and larger than the biblical authors realized. The ancients knew of no number larger than "thousands" and had no word for billion, let alone light-year. The universe is far more vast than they realized, and it stands to reason that the God they imagined as its Creator is different as well.

We know that several versions of the Flood story were told in Near Eastern antiquity. The gods in those accounts varied considerably from the God we meet in the Bible. The Bible describes God as acting out of moral concern—bringing down a catastrophic flood in order to stop earthly violence. After the fact, God regrets the mass drowning and creates the rainbow to remind humanity that he will not do it again.[3]

Literary and archeological evidence suggests that a great flood did, in fact, occur in ancient Mesopotamia. But was it really caused by a God intent on punishing wrongdoers? Was there really just one righteous man whose family merited saving? Did God really say he would never do it again? Is this really why there are rainbows? Or is all this a narrative expression of the ancient religious imagination? By now, our answer should be clear.

We see something similar in Leviticus, where people with various dermatological ailments are instructed to consult a priest.[4] Today we know that a physician is a better choice. Skin rashes are the product of microbial infection, not sinful misconduct. But as in the Flood story, the biblical authors portrayed the link as causal. Their likely intent was to prod us into leading better lives. We can appreciate that, but if the story so motivates us, it is because the narrative has power, not because God actually works in that way.

We also know now that human sacrifice was not unusual in ancient Canaan. This puts God's seemingly incomprehensible request to Abraham to sacrifice his son in historical context. It was

3. Genesis 8:21; Genesis 9:12–16.
4. Leviticus 13:2–57.

not necessarily cruelty or madness on the part of either God or Abraham—it was a reflection of the practices of the day.

Such lessons of science and scholarship can help us clarify some of what God is not. God did not create our world just six thousand years ago. God did not bring a great flood to wipe out most of humanity because people were behaving badly. God does not want us to have skin rashes examined by religious functionaries. God does not test our faith by asking us to kill innocents.

## GOD AND UNIVERSAL LAWS

Some speculate that God does not act to prevent evil, injustice, or calamity because God does not know, does not care, or both. If either of these is true, then God is not much of a God.

Others say God does not intervene so that we learn to work things out for ourselves. If this is the case, history shows that the threshold for divine intervention is so high as to be effectively nonexistent.

There is also the possibility that injustices in this world are made right by God in the next one. As we've noted, while there is no evidence for this, many people are nonetheless sustained by the belief. But those of us who are unwilling to live with the expectation that wrongs in this world will somehow be made right in the next require something more.

Science makes the case that it is not possible for God to intervene as the Bible describes and that God is bound by the same universal laws as the rest of us. If we can accept this, it allows us to acknowledge that things happen because of human intention, physics, circumstance, and luck. Events, be they tragic or ordinary, are the result of natural, logical, or random causes—not supernatural manipulation.

## CONCLUSIONS ON GOD AND JUSTICE

All this now allows us to ask, and answer, some essential questions:

1. *Is Divine Justice lacking in our world because God does not actively implement it?*

   Yes. The principles of justice are flouted unceasingly, while our constant and desperate pleas for God to remedy the situation go unheeded. Injustice is far too abundant to claim otherwise.

2. *Is Divine Justice lacking because we are somehow not deserving of it?*

   Yes and no. We can say that there are universal laws of justice which, when violated, carry consequences for those who violate them. But this occurs as a manifestation of the God of Law and Spirit, not because the God of some religious traditions is withholding it from us.

3. *Who, besides us, is capable of bringing Justice about?*

   No one. God's Spirit may include the spirit of justice, but God needs us to establish it in the world. God only asks us to do what is right.[5] We receive only as much justice as we earn—and we can earn only so much.

§

Justice is not a matter of luck or *karma*. It is not a matter of everything working out in the end. It is not a matter of mystery. It is a matter of recognizing that it is our job to apply as much of God's Spirit to the world as we possibly can.

5. Heschel, *God in Search of Man*, 376.

# 12

# What God Is—Or Might Be

SCIENCE AND SCHOLARSHIP CAN also help us apprehend what God is. They teach that the universe is governed by certain immutable laws. We know that if we intend to live well—or for that matter to live at all—we need to live in harmony with those laws. We also appreciate that body, mind, spirit, and society thrive best when we do.

We can likewise understand these laws to be aspects of God. We can view biblical narratives, legal and otherwise, as our ancestors' attempts to identify and live in concert with them. There are many scriptural descriptions of how God acts and what God wants that are consistent with the spirit we've described here as divine. There are others that are not.

The numerous biblical narratives that portray God as either harming or benefiting particular individuals, groups or nations fall into the latter category. Such activity cannot be reconciled with the laws of the universe.

There is no evidence that exceptions to these laws were ever granted to any individuals, members of a specific ethnic tribe, or practitioners of a particular faith—much less at the behest of a specific deity. Nor will we find any. Beliefs that such occurrences took place are best understood, once again, as narrative expressions of the religious imagination.

## MEETING GOD

So how do we meet this God who is one with universal law? Our starting point remains the Bible. In it, God regularly shows caring and kindness to those he favors. But we don't need the Bible to tell us that caring and kindness are among life's highest blessings. People, animals, and, it is said, even plants respond to them. Caring and kindness are considered holy in every faith. We can allow that these qualities are part of the makeup of the God of Law and Spirit.

We can envision a God who is one with the laws of nature, physics and the universe—which include the laws of caring, kindness, and love. We can envision a God who does not favor any particular tribe, nation, or group of believers because of their creed or ethnic identity. We can approach biblical accounts that portray God acting in that way as we would any other narrative. It may contain worthwhile lessons and value, just not necessarily ultimate lessons and value.

We can envision a God whose essence is spirit, and we can bring that spirit to life through acts of kindness, justice, and love. The more we practice them, the more we bring God's presence into the world. As we do, we grow in godliness.

## VIOLENCE AND LOVE—
## IN CREATION AND IN US

For some time now, science has subscribed to the Big Bang theory of creation. It holds that a singular burst of violent energy gave birth to the universe nearly fourteen billion years ago. Matter was scattered in every direction. The matter and energy created then are said to pulse through each of us today.

Interestingly, the Big Bang theory is not inconsistent with the familiar biblical account: "God said, 'Let there be light, and there was light."[1] Of course, the scriptural authors and their classical interpreters had no understanding of the Big Bang. But that there was violence in Creation and particularly, in us, the created, they understood very well.

There is also love in us. Perhaps that came from the Big Bang, too. Either way, we know that human life would be unimaginable without it. Any system of understanding God, humanity, and the universe needs to account for love. It is not by accident that God is spoken of as loving and compassionate in every great faith.

Our love and God's love may be powerful, but they are not all-powerful. They exist in tension with creation's violence. Sometimes love prevails, sometimes violence does.

We have some say in determining the outcome of that struggle, at least as far as our own lives are concerned. We can work to become more loving, caring, and compassionate, or we can allow ourselves to become vengeful and cruel.

It is an article of faith that when we build our lives on a foundation of love, we receive support from the divine spirit of love in return. If we choose to live a life of violence, that spirit can dominate us just as easily. But even when we build our lives on love, violent bolts from the blue can find us. Random calamity, accident, or illness can upend any life, no matter how well lived.

1. Genesis 1:3.

# A GOD WE CAN HAVE

It is essential to recognize that though God's spirit may be strong, it can be overpowered by violence, disease, and random disaster. This does not mean that caring, kindness, justice and love—and the God in whom these spirits live—are not real. It does mean that they are not almighty.

God's spirit of goodness can also fall victim to forces of evil and destruction. That spirit does not prevail if there are not enough people actively working to carry out God's will. The Rabbinic teaching that if we do not act as God's witnesses, it is as if there is no God[2], is not merely a simile, it is a truth.

The fact that the divine spirits of love and caring are sometimes defeated by hatred, cruelty, and violence does not mean that God is not real. It simply means that God and goodness do not win every battle. It means that good people can be harmed by others exercising their own free will. It means that the God of Law and Spirit is one with, and does not overturn, the laws of the universe.

This God of Law and Spirit may not be all the God we want. But it is a God we can have. It is a God whose roots we find in Scripture. It is a God whose spirit we can touch with acts of kindness, love, and justice. It is a God who acts neither imperiously nor unjustly.

Because it makes no sense to ask this God for what is not possible, e.g., to shield us from the effects of the laws of physics, this is a God we will not think of as having failed us in times of loss. Accordingly, this is a God who can pass the Tragedy Test.

§

The God of Law and Spirit is one with whom we can maintain a relationship. It is a God who asks us to be more than we have been.

The God of Law and Spirit is neither an all-powerful God nor a no-god. It is a God who remains a moral counsel and force for justice. It is a God we can live with and live for.

2. *Op. cit., Sifrei* Deuteronomy 346.

## DOING WHAT WE CAN

"Justice, justice shall you pursue."
—DEUTERONOMY 16:20

There is clearly a certain order in our world. There is also a certain amount of horror. Part of whatever order there is works to ensure that good is rewarded. Most of us have faith that—to some degree at least—goodness is rewarded by the world, by our fellow human beings, and by the resulting quality of life in people who pursue it.

We can and should continue to do as much good as we can. It will not protect us from everything, but it is something upon which an honorable life can be built. We should not do it for the rewards it may bring or because we think it will immunize us from suffering. We should do it because it is right. We should do it because it is the best we can do.

## ACCEPTING WHAT WE MUST

"Success is not final. Failure is not fatal.
It is the courage to continue that counts."
—WINSTON CHURCHILL

The faith that acting rightly, and often enough, brings blessing remains no less true after a loss than it was before. Acting rightly has the power to set us on a course that is both rewarding and praiseworthy. Still, it is not an absolute. We can be ensnared in the storms of history.[3] We can be killed in an accident, caught in an earthquake, or fall victim to a disease for which there is no cure.

At the same time success, and the blessings that come with it, can be determined by many factors. Wealth can accumulate through hard work, by dint of good fortune, or through nefarious means. And we know that hard work is not always rewarded with prosperity. To say that the God of Justice desires such outcomes would make for an awkward faith indeed.

---

3. The number of civilian casualties in modern wars greatly outnumber military casualties—which themselves are in the scores of millions.

## SOLVING MYSTERIES

If we can acknowledge that God is neither mysterious nor cruel, we can likewise posit that God is not a Heavenly Director.

It is possible that God has only established the rules, and it is our job to discern how to live within them. It is possible that justice is entirely up to us. It is possible that the God we imagine as all-just and all-directing is not really God at all.

It is possible that answering the question, "How could this happen?" is not beyond our capability. It is possible that things happen, good and bad, for no reason other than the laws of nature require that they do.

Belief in the God who is one with the laws of nature and the spirit of holiness can solve many of faith's otherwise intractable mysteries. At the same time, it can give us a God who is a faithful partner, not an unpredictable adversary. It can give us divine justice as something to work for, not wait for. It can give us meaning in the lives we create. It can give us concrete truth instead of imagined fantasy.

It can also give an answer to the question, "Why did Tali die?" It was an accident—one that can be explained in its entirety by the laws of physics, the laws of nature, and the laws of God as sages such as Maimonides, Spinoza, and others have understood them.

## A FAITH FOR GROWN-UPS

"Truth is that which works."[4]
—John Dewey

It may not be easy to transition our faith to a God who offers us more cold truth than warm comfort. But when it comes to challenging established understandings of how the Almighty works, we are on familiar religious, and certainly Jewish, ground.

Moses stood up to God—and prevailed—when he argued it would be wrong to destroy the Israelites after their various sins in the wilderness.[5] The Talmudic Rabbis debated whether it would have been better if God had not created humanity in the first place. They concluded it would have been better if he had not.[6] In later centuries, pious Jews in the *shtetls* (small villages) and concentration camps of Europe put God on mock trial. He was most often found guilty.

It is possible that God is not all we think God is, nor all that we want God to be. Perhaps the God we imagine is not the all-powerful God of the entire universe but instead the more limited God of cosmic sector 2∑CX986Γ—or some such?[7] And what if the God of "our sector" is merely a limited aspect of a greater God still?

Whether we choose to look at God with flaws and shortcomings, as underachieving or unjust, the limits are there for all to see. We may not have all the answers, but the available evidence points to a God that cannot—or does not—do nearly as much as we wish God would.

Understanding God as Law and Spirit helps us here. The God who is Law and Spirit will not be the target of our anger or disappointment when things do not go as we expect they should. The God of Law and Spirit can be on our side, with support,

4. Kelly, *Education and Democracy*, 66.

5. Exodus 32:7–14; Numbers 14:13–19.

6. *Babylonian Talmud, Eruvin* 13b.

7. Idea shared by H. George Kagan, Esq.

encouragement, and love through thick and thin. The God of Law and Spirit can partner with us in repairing and civilizing the world.

The God of Law and Spirit is not responsible for everything that happens. The God of Law and Spirit is a God for grown-ups.

# 13

# Prayer and Ritual Through the God of Law and Spirit

## PRAYERS THAT MAKE SENSE

PRAYER IS THE TRADITIONAL way in which people seek to approach God. Prayer can be public or private, communal or individual. But in order for prayer to be meaningful, it needs to cohere with the God we seek to address. Attempts to draw near to a God we conceive of as universal force and spirit will, of necessity, be different from attempts to approach a God we imagine as a personal responder.

If we do not believe that God has the ability to reach down from heaven and protect us, prayers asking God to do so will strike us as awkward, at best. If God has no power to grant our individual requests, making such prayers can pull us further away from the divine spirit instead of closer to it.

If, on the other hand, we believe that God's essence is the spirit of righteousness, love, kindness, and truth, we can use our prayer to make more of those qualities our own. If enough people in a society do this, they will gain real strength and power. This, in turn, can help bring about a measure of the protection we seek. A society in which the divine spirit of goodness is strong will be safer than one in which it is not.

Still, that spirit has only so much power. It will not alter the laws of nature, no matter how fervently we plead for it to do so.

However, that spirit can do much else. It can deepen and enrich our personal and professional relationships. It can take root in our work. It can guide us along a healing path. It can help us set a moral compass.

Unfortunately, our relationship with God, whatever it may be, will not protect us or our loved ones from untimely death, disease, misfortune, war, or natural disaster. To pretend otherwise almost assures that both we and our God will have a hard time passing the Tragedy Test when we face it.

§

Instead of making our prayer a series of requests to a spirit that has no power to grant them, it may be better to pray with the intention of touching the divine around us and within us.

Prayer can be an attempt to express awe at the grandeur of nature. It can be meditative, listening for the still, small voice within.[1] It can be part of a search for the path that leads to our highest selves.

There are typically modest quantities of such prayers in traditional public worship. More often, we see scripts that suggest a supernatural God with intervening powers and, on occasion, a fearsome personality. In many prayer books though, we also find offerings intended as guides to help us strengthen those spirits of justice, love, and kindness.

Composers of liturgy and leaders of public worship are well aware of this tension. Given that few, if any, pleas to God are demonstrably answered, we are told they are nonetheless important because they remind us what is important to ask for. That point is reasonable enough. But understanding God as Law and Spirit encourages us to offer prayers and meditations that:

1. I Kings 19:12.

- facilitate our attempts to encounter the ever-present divine presence.

- emphasize that God's spirit is made concrete through acts of goodness, love, and charity.

- fashion the narratives of our particular faith in service to these ends.[2]

- remind us that God is more concerned with righteousness than with ritual.[3]

- recognize that prayer is meant to change our course of action, not God's.

At the same time, it may be better for our spiritual development to forego prayers that:

- call upon God to intervene in our affairs or respond to us personally.

- claim that God enters history in order to grant victory to one people over another.

- declare an overly privileged relationship between God and any nation, tribe, or specific community.

- proclaim division, triumphalism, or hatred.

- depict God as overturning the laws of nature.

Our public worship and private prayers serve us best when they facilitate—rather than conspire against—the highest understanding of God we can grasp.

---

2. For example, Jews can invoke the Exodus, Christians the life and death of Jesus, Muslims spiritual *jihad*, etc. All can teach that their particular histories are meant to strengthen the universal values of justice, love, freedom, and service.

3. Isaiah 58:5–7: "This is the fast I desire: To loose the chains of wickedness and undo the bands of the yoke to let the oppressed go free . . . It is to share your bread with the hungry, and to take the poor into your home; when you see the naked, to clothe him, and not to ignore your own kin."

## RITUAL AND ITS ROLE

"Religion isn't what you believe, it is what you do."[4]
—ROBERT N. BELLAH

In every faith, ritual is part of what people do. When we engage in ritual, we are attempting to draw nearer to the God we wish to serve and strengthen that relationship. At its best, religious ritual pulls us closer to holiness.

In the Bible, God's first question to Adam is "Where are you?"[5] A commentary suggests that God is not asking for one ancient man's physical location. Rather, God is posing an existential question to each of us, i.e., "Where are you—right now—on your journey through life?"

From this we can derive corollary questions. Where are you—in your efforts to:

- improve the world?
- relieve suffering and diminish corruption?
- protect the weak from the predations of the strong?
- honor the gift of life you've been given?
- nurture the spirit of gratitude within you?
- become a better human being?

If religion is what we do, one of ritual's goals should be to help us better respond to such questions. If ritual is where human meets divine, its role is to strengthen the relationship between the two. If a particular ritual does not do this, we should reconsider its value—or the spirit in which we are practicing it.

4. Bellah (1927–2013), was an American scholar known for his work on the sociology of religion.

5. Genesis 3:9.

## HOW MUCH IS ENOUGH?

Since all faiths mandate that we treat our fellow human beings ethically, we can adjudge the biblical verses that prescribe such behavior (e.g., give charity, judge fairly, etc.) to be worthwhile and enduring. This is true whether God is limited or unlimited, personal or non-personal, even whether or not we believe God exists.

The relationship between us and the ritual prescriptions designed to mediate our interactions with God is more complex.

If God exists and does not protect us, even if we are meticulous in our ritual practice, we can be forgiven for asking why we should bother. Why should we keep our end of the Sacred Agreement[6] if the other party does not? And if God does not exist, or does not exist with the ability to notice our personal ritual behavior or lack thereof, why are we troubling ourselves in the first place?

There are various ways to answer these questions. First of all, ritual can play an important role in shaping family and community. A community grounded in ritual can be of tremendous aid to someone who is pursuing a spiritual path. In the words of Robert Bellah, "You will never understand God unless you are involved in some kind of community where that word begins to make sense in the life of that community."[7]

Whether we agree with Bellah or not, there are other reasons to practice. Ritual is a way to ensure that there is a meaningful, ongoing place in our lives for God. Ritual can instill and reinforce the understanding that a well-lived life is about more than what matters to us personally. Ritual can make us more aware of our obligations to others. Ritual can be a part of our spiritual discipline. Ritual can help us fine-tune our personal behavior.

But if our ritual practice is not anything that God is noticing, much less altering his behavior in response to, it carries less of a moral imperative than, say, the mandate to treat the powerless with respect and decency.

---

6. Essentially: do what I ask and I will take care of you.

7. Joas, *Conversation*, 6.

Whether or not we observe a particular ritual does not affect the actions of the God we have described as universal Law and Spirit. If our observance has a positive effect on our own morality and spirituality, then that is where its value lies.

If we understand this, the next question becomes: how much ritual do we require to remind ourselves that what God wants from us most is justice, service, and peace? Some of us may do better with frequent reminders. If so, there are sufficient ritual opportunities in every faith to help us meet that need. Others who require fewer may find that a different quantity of observance can facilitate a consecrated journey as well.

## REALLY?

People who care about perpetuating their faith would do well to consider that some rituals can drive people away from, instead of towards, a life of deeper religious commitment. When a ritual is seen as intellectually or morally flawed, it does just that.

Look into a traditional prayer book, in its original language if possible, cast a thoughtful eye, and see how many times you are moved to ask the question, "Really?"

The book likely suggests that God extends special protection to the faithful. Really? It may imply that those who practice its particular faith are favored—over and above those who do not. Really? It may even suggest that indiscriminate slaughter in God's name is, or has been, sanctioned under various circumstances. Really?

Of course, not really. Yet, there are numerous texts in every Western faith that imply these very things.

While it is true that too meager a ritual life may impede our spiritual growth, it is also true that ritual repetition of false or misleading statements and practices will not nurture it either.

The actual value of ritual is the degree to which it puts us in touch with the spirit of the divine and moves us to embrace it. The God of Law and Spirit does not find us wanting for ritual infractions. The measure of the divine presence in our lives is the amount of goodness, love, and holiness we create. To the extent that ritual strengthens these impulses within us, it is beneficial. To the extent that it ignores or weakens them, it is either empty, counterproductive, or both.

# PART III—ACCEPTANCE

# 14

# No Way Around It
# but Through It

MY CHILDHOOD, ADOLESCENCE, AND early adulthood left me with
the impression that while the world could definitely be a dangerous place, it was, by and large, a benevolent one. We were taught
that if we worked honestly and diligently, reward would come to
us in due course. If we were sensible and took reasonable care of
ourselves, most of life's hazards could be avoided.

This worldview made sense for me, who had the good fortune
to grow up in stable middle-class surroundings, the first-born son
of loving parents, and a member of a devoted extended family. I
lived in a community that invested in its children and was provided with good schools, parks, values, and opportunities. All this
in a United States of America that was at a high water mark of its
power and prosperity. It combined to make me feel pretty secure.
A head-on collision with tragedy was the last thing I expected. It
was probably the last thing Tali expected as well.

Other people, blessed with similar talents, work ethic, and
moral code, but who grew up in less fortunate circumstances, may
have developed a different outlook altogether. For many of God's
children, the possibility of tragedy is not remote, it is ever-present.

If we are going to speak about acceptance, let's begin by accepting this: circumstance and luck play a major role in determining

the course of our lives and the course of our faith. When we are secure in our lives, it is much easier to feel secure in our faith.

But bolts out of the blue strike good people, too—not because they deserve it or because God has it in for them—but because the laws of nature and circumstance are largely oblivious to one's character. If we insist on believing otherwise, our path to acceptance will be longer and rockier.

## "LIFE GOES ON"
## AND
## "IT IS WHAT IT IS"

"Life goes on." It has become a routine response to loss of almost any kind. Your team loses the big game; life goes on. Your candidate loses the election; life goes on. Your country loses the war; life goes on.

More personally, our marriage fails; life goes on. We become injured or incapacitated; life goes on. We lose our job; life goes on. We lose a loved one; life goes on.

A companion phrase is, "It is what it is." It advises us, Zen-like, to make peace with whatever difficulty or disappointment is at hand. Because after all, what is, is reality.

Familiar as these sayings have become, if we are unable to accept the truths they contain, our recovery from trauma will be slowed. We may remain burdened and despondent, states in which we can ill afford to linger. If we are fighting against reality, it is best to remember that reality is holding all of the high cards.

Faith has a role to play here. Faith can give us the courage to go on. Faith can help us regain the strength to make life worth living. Faith after loss, like life itself, will not be the same as it was before. But faith can give us spiritual perspectives that will help us heal.

Faith is a living organism. Like a broken bone, it can be reset and mended. But we need to give it the opportunity to do so—especially after a loss. If we want to recover our lives, if we want to recover our faith, we need to recover our ability to accept that "it is what is" and "life goes on."

## ACCEPTING JUDGMENT

We noted earlier that it is a Jewish custom, upon hearing news of a death, to offer the words, "Blessed is the true Judge." On certain ritual occasions, I choose to render the original Hebrew as, "Blessed is the One whose judgments are true."

It is more than a change to the passive voice. The first formulation casts God as heavenly judge, jury and, as it were, executioner—decreeing our deaths for whatever his reasons might be. The latter describes a God more consistent with the one we have described here as the God of Law and Spirit. But both expressions set acceptance as the goal of mourning.

We cannot heal, even partially, until and unless we are able to accept our losses—emotionally and spiritually. In order to reach acceptance, we need to be grateful for what was and cherish the legacy that remains. If we rail against what is no more, or can never be again, we will not heal.

## HEALING COMES FROM PRESENCE

"Wisdom is found in the house of mourning."
—ECCLESIASTES 7:4

Jewish tradition teaches that when visiting a house of mourning, it is preferable not to speak to the mourner until and unless the mourner speaks to us first. The teaching reflects the awareness that on such occasions, our presence likely says more than our words possibly can. It also reflects the understanding that whatever words we do share will likely be inadequate.

The eminent Rabbi Abraham Joshua Heschel once flew from New York to Boston to visit the home of a colleague in mourning. He arrived at the house, sat silently for an hour, then rose, left for the airport, and went home. Without speaking a word, his presence conveyed support, comfort, and strength.[1]

§

We received hundreds of communications containing thousands of words after Talia died. They came from near and far, from family and colleagues, from our friends, from her friends, and from people we hadn't heard from in years. So many of them tried—and failed—to express the "right words." They did not fail because they were unskilled at speaking or writing. They failed because no such words exist.

Why don't they? Perhaps it's like this. When we lose a loved one, we lose a part of our personal world—the world we live in most of the time, the world that revolves around us. Our personal world is the world in which we attempt to bring our values, hopes, and aspirations to life. The larger world can seem remote, uncaring, and immovable. Most of us establish our individual identity in our personal world.

---

1. Story shared by Rabbi Jack Riemer, who accompanied Rabbi Heschel on the visit.

We construct these worlds on multiple foundations. Typically, they include work, friendship, charitable activity, leisure pursuits, etc. But at the heart of most personal worlds is the family.

When we lose a member of the family, our personal world is rocked. The jolt is exponentially worse if we lose a child. We invest innumerable hours of love and devotion in the growth and development of our children. In addition to residing at the center of their own world, they are part of the foundation of ours. Losing them upends us, as perhaps nothing else does.

There is the shock, horror, and tragedy of a young life filled with promise suddenly ended. It is accompanied by an almost comic sense of cruelty. Our sacred efforts have been crushed, even mocked. It is a bitter joke—and no one is laughing.

Recovery can begin when we accept, that even with all this, our efforts were not futile. If a child leaves anything of a legacy, and Talia certainly did, then that lives on. Brief as it was, her life was not in vain—and neither were our efforts as parents. It was important for us to take this to heart.

It is why every visit, every attempt at consolation, every name at the bottom of every card and screen, every voice at the other end of every call—no matter how inadequate the words may have been—meant everything to us. Those names and that presence meant far more than whatever "right words" they were searching to find.

We understood that they were trying to say something like this:

We know that nothing can replace what you have lost. We understand that your personal world will never be the same. But we want you to know that we are part of that world as well—and we will remain so.

You have lost something infinite, but you have not lost everything. You have not lost us. You have not lost our caring. You have not lost the goodness that has come from your efforts. You have not lost the goodness that came from hers. Your life and your personal world, in spite of this tragedy, remains one of great value. Please try to remember this.

None of this cured. All of it helped. I shudder to think where we would have been without it.

§

If you absolutely feel that you must say something to a mourner, the words "I can't imagine" may be as good as any. Even if you've been through something that seems similar, chances are, it's not the same for the other person as it was for you. It's true—we really *can't* imagine. And we don't even want to try.

## MY WAGER

Not enjoyment, and not sorrow,
Is our destined end or way;
But to act, that each to-morrow
Find us farther than to-day.[2]
—HENRY WADSWORTH LONGFELLOW

Following Tali's death, a friend shared with me his faith's understanding that there is no such thing as "before one's time." He said she must have done all that she was meant to do in this world for God to have brought her into the next. I was touched by his caring and his belief—but I could not accept his words.

His faith, once again, presupposes an all-powerful and all-just God who chooses to inflict suffering upon us for reasons known but to him. It also depends on the existence of a world after this one in which perfect justice reigns. My friend understands and accepts this. But if that is what is necessary to maintain faith in a God who is all-powerful and all-good—and it is—it is for me, at least at this point, a bridge too far.

It can be comforting, and perhaps even harmless, to trust that the goodness we accomplish on earth will be rewarded in a world beyond this one. But it requires an active religious imagination to do so. As far as we know for certain, the only world and the only life that may actually exist "under God" is this one here.

It would be soothing to believe that we somehow journey to a world of perfect justice after we leave this one. It may even give us the strength we need to carry on. But we have no evidence that any such place exists.[3]

Blaise Pascal, the seventeenth-century French philosopher, wrestled with the idea of an afterlife and offered a proposition that

2. Longfellow, *Psalm*, 4.

3. Interestingly, the idea of a next world of restorative justice entered Judeo-Christian thought during the period of major Hellenistic influence. This era began in the late fourth century BCE, well after both the traditional and scholarly dates for the completion of the Torah.

came to be known as Pascal's wager. It hinges on the contention that none of us can, using reason, either prove or disprove God's existence. According to Pascal, it is, therefore, better to live as if there is a God. If we are right, we will receive the promised heavenly reward. If we are wrong, we are no worse off than we would have been before.

Pascal's wager is based on a Christian understanding of the God who rewards and punishes in the next world. Within those parameters, his argument is compelling.

It is also possible to wager that there is no such afterlife, while at the same time doing our best to bring a greater quantity of justice to this world. If we are mistaken, and there is a next world overseen by a just God, we will be pleasantly surprised by whatever awaits us there. If it turns out there is no life beyond this one, we will have made the most of our time here. I'm calling this proposition Agler's wager, and I invite you to join me in it.

## ETERNAL LIFE?

In place of the belief in a physical next world, bodily resurrection, reincarnation, etc., some moderns instead embrace the principle of the soul's immortality. The belief traces back at least to classical Greek civilization and we see it today in liturgical statements such as "God has implanted eternal life within us" and "the dust returns to the earth as the spirit lives on with God who gave it."

What actually happens to our soul is left unspecified, as it must be. None of us knows what, if anything, lies beyond the world we inhabit. But instead of promising a bodily life after this one, which strikes many as fantastical, the affirmation that the human soul is eternal is more spiritual, vague though it be, can still give us hope.

It can also give us meaning. The teaching that each of us possesses a soul that is eternal, godly, and indestructible says that we are more than mere flesh and blood. It says that the mythical breath of life that God blew into Adam's nostrils gives our humanity both divinity and infinite worth.[4]

Do we really live on after this life? Undoubtedly we live on in the memories we have created and in the good deeds we have authored. Beyond that, it remains a mystery.

---

4. Genesis 2:7 The Hebrew word for breath that appears here, *ruach*-רוח, is also used as an expression for soul.

## ON GRIEVING

It is a Jewish tradition to cover the mirrors in a house of mourning. The customary explanation is that it is not the time to be preoccupied with everyday vanities. The mirror covers are removed after one week. The period of grieving often lasts well beyond.

Every faith has a ritual mourning calendar that may or may not correspond with our personal emotional calendar. Particularly after a traumatic loss, we may require more time than our tradition prescribes. All the while, professional and social obligations prevent us from making too public a show of sorrow. In society today, there is often pressure to be positive, upbeat, and cheerful.

How do we mourn under such circumstances? For the sake of our inner well-being, we should work to find a way. Houses of worship offer opportunities. So do periods of solitude and meditation, as well as counselors and support groups. Healing from loss can be a long-term undertaking. The more severe the loss, the longer the recovery is likely to take. We should not pretend to be further along than we are.

The aftermath of loss is a good time to avoid mirrors of whatever description. It may be best to turn down invitations extended to "cheer us up." It can be advisable to refrain from social engagements that will not facilitate our recuperation. There are no shortcuts when it comes to healing—neither for a broken bone nor a wounded soul.

## A SIX-STEP PROGRAM

Working through grief can be compared to working through a twelve-step program. There are chapters of Alcoholics Anonymous, Narcotics Anonymous, Overeaters Anonymous, and many others in cities and towns around the world. Mourners Anonymous? Not so much. Although there may be fewer recognized roadmaps and supportive communities, working through complex grief can require at least as much determination as overcoming a harmful addiction.

Once again, professional counselors and support groups can be of great assistance. I recommend them for people whose grieving is especially painful. Hearing the stories of others who have suffered similarly can make us realize that as intense and personal as our own loss may be, we are not alone. Simply listening empathetically can be invaluable. Others are on the path to recovery and we can be, too.

In the meantime, for all who mourn, I offer this modest Six-Step Program:

*Step 1:* I will accept what is.

*Step 2:* I will be grateful for what was.

*Step 3:* I will honor, in thought and action, the memories that endure.

*Step 4:* I will avoid self-pity.

*Step 5:* I will find a way to forgive them, and us, for whatever happened.

*Step 6:* I will seek love and support from family, friends, and faith.

As with all such programs, the steps need to be worked. I wish you strength as you walk the walk.

## WELL-GROUNDED FAITH

"May you have a strong foundation
when the winds of changes shift."[5]
—Bob Dylan

As we noted at the outset, most of us believe that life should be fair. If we are honest, hardworking and kind, we expect a measure of peace, prosperity, and security in return. We have been taught that this is the God-ordained order of things. There are indeed times when life works out this way. When it does, our faith is strengthened. When it doesn't, our faith is tested.

If we are going to emerge from the trauma of what we consider an unfair loss with faith intact, our core beliefs need to pass the Tragedy Test.

In the wake of Talia's death, I have concluded that for me at least, the following faith principles are valid. They are foundations upon which a meaningful life and a living faith can be reset. They facilitate acceptance and healing. They can give us the power to bless ourselves and those around us with strength and holiness.

It is good to:

- Do good for its own sake.

- Live as if God commands us to pursue justice and peace.

- Show kindness unconditionally.

- Refrain from doing to others what we would not want done to us (The Golden Rule).

- Speak truth to power. (Heaven knows it needs to hear it.)

- Limit our words to those that are true, necessary, and fair.

- Be an active learner in pursuit of greater understanding.

- Commit to a discipline that facilitates personal and spiritual growth.

5. *Forever Young*, 1973

- Center life around service that is grounded in higher purpose.

- Attempt to be an exemplary member of your faith—it brings honor and respect.

- Hold onto hope.

There are also a number of ideas that I no longer accept. They include the beliefs that:

- God extends special protection to his faithful.

- Offering prayerful petitions encourages God to work on our behalf.

- God intervenes in our private, communal, or historical lives.

- God is concerned with the particular details of our ritual practice.

- Every word of ancient Scripture is the highest we can know.

At the same time we can conclude that we do not give our lives meaning by saying we believe in—or do not believe in—any specific understanding of God. We give our lives meaning through the work we accomplish—or attempt to accomplish—and the love we create.

# 15

# Happiness After Loss

AFTER BEING STRUCK BY violence, chaos or evil, happiness can seem distant. So can a living God. Can we respond to life's worst without losing our own best? To say, "I trust in God's spirit of goodness," particularly after a painful loss, requires faith and courage. Taken together, they give us a chance to be happy again.

## HAPPY ALL THE TIME?

"It is a great virtue[1] to be happy at all times." A sect of Jews have made this statement by their founder, Rabbi Nachman of Bratslav (1772–1810), into something of a credo. It is worth pondering.

The news from the wider world is frequently depressing. Tragedy strikes countless numbers of God's children every day. Corruption is abundant in all its forms. Our bodies begin deteriorating all too quickly. Sorrow and loss eventually find each of us. Given all this, how is it possible to be happy all the time?

Part of the solution may be to accept with gratitude what is, and to refrain from being miserable over what is not, can never be, or can never be again.

§

1. Literally, "commandment."

I have known my share of parents who have gone through serious crises with children—or for that matter, with one another. At times, extraordinary counseling or care was indicated. Still, neither the diagnosis nor its aftermath was always handled well. Recrimination, substance abuse, and even marriage dissolution were not unknown.

Years later, some came to understand that it would have been better to be accepting, and even grateful for what was, rather than to bewail what was not, or could not be. To their undying credit, there are people who are able to make this journey. So many fall victim to self-pity and never recover. But in spite of the scars, new beginnings are possible. It is fair to say that even veterans of journeys like this, can be happy people.

§

To be happy all the time does not necessarily mean that we are joyful at every moment. Nor does it mean that painful trials will not take their toll.

It does mean that when calamity finds us, acceptance can give us at least some of the strength we need to overcome it. It also means that if we are able to focus on gratitude and love for what is, instead of despairing over what is not, our chances to achieve happiness are commensurately greater.

## IMAGES OF HAPPINESS

People often say they feel pressured by images, both from the mass media and now today, from social media. It is no wonder. The mass media typically showcases people who are—or at least appear to be—beautiful and prosperous. (That's how they get us to look at them.) On social media, we share images that, more often than not, show us as "happy all the time."

But as we know, every life has more than its share of non-cheerful moments. Times of loss are among them. Loss makes us realize that life, at its root, is about much more than looking happy. True happiness is deeper and less fleeting than any image of the moment can convey.

Even if we are carrying deep sadness within, it remains possible to be a happy person. Philosopher Søren Kierkegaard's wisdom that "the door to happiness opens outwards," i.e., we find it when we extend ourselves on behalf of others, can be especially helpful to remember.

## HAPPINESS WITH PEACE

"The way to be happy is to make someone happy and
make a little heaven down here."[2]
—Sunday school song

Many prayer books contain a meditation to the effect that, "Peace is God's most precious gift."

We are so often not at peace—with one another, with ourselves, or with the world around us. When tragedy strikes an undeserving soul, especially someone who is near and dear to us, it can upend whatever sense of peace and happiness we do have.

It can be a challenge to not let ourselves be undone by personal tragedy. When Tali died, I resolved that I was not going to allow myself, or if I could help it, anyone else in my family, become an additional victim. I had no idea how I might do this, or if it was even possible. But I knew that I was going to try.

Fortunately, I had faith to draw upon. Faith reminds us that there was blessing before, and it reassures us that there will be blessing again. Faith can help put an emotional floor underneath us.

Faith also teaches that when we act rightly, it is honorable in itself, honorable in the eyes of others and honorable in the eyes of God.[3] When we act rightly, and often enough, it can restore at least some measure of the peace and happiness that we have lost.

Faith can be tenuous, but there are times when it is validated. Doing good, in harmony with the teachings of the God who is Law and Spirit, whether we win or lose, whether we prevail or not, can be an essential component of recovery from loss.

2. I first heard this sung at the Talia Agler Girls Shelter in Nairobi, Kenya.
3. after *Mishnah Avot* 2:1.

# 16

# Nevertheless

"It is not for you to complete the work,
but neither are you free to abstain from it."[1]
—RABBI TARFON

THE PHRASE AF AL *pi chen* has its origin in classical Hebrew and it
remains in use today. We can translate it as "in spite of everything"
or "nevertheless." It is an empowering response to life's inevitable
injustices.[2]

Even though goodness is not always rewarded as it should
be—or even as much of the Bible says it will be—we can *neverthe-*
*less* affirm its value and place it at the center of our lives. We do not
do this in order to receive some potential heavenly reward. We do
this because it is the best we can do. We do this in order that we
might become a source of even greater blessing.[3]

§

1. *Mishnah Avot* 2:21.

2. "Nevertheless say yes to life," is similarly offered by Viktor Frankl in
*Man's Search for Meaning.* See below.

3. after *Mishnah Avot* 4:2.

No one has yet to prove or disprove, logically and scientifically, whether or not God exists. Which is why we call belief in God faith.

In this world, there are things we know and things we don't know. There are surely things we will never know. Rather than attempting to prove what we cannot, it may be best, in the meantime, to devote ourselves to what we can know and accomplish.[4]

We know that the world desperately needs our healing efforts. Whether God exists or not, or is of one nature or another, is almost beside this point. Each of us can, in words attributed to St. Augustine, "Pray as if everything depends on God. Act as if everything depends on you."

Even absent proof, the quality of human life improves demonstrably when we *nevertheless* act as if a living God commands us to fulfill the words of the prophet by doing justly, loving mercy, and living with humility.[5]

4. after Deuteronomy 29:28.

5. Micah 6:8.

## SURELY?

The words of the Twenty-Third psalm are as well known as any in the Bible. We often hear them recited publicly, particularly at memorial services. Individuals seeking strength and solace contemplate them privately. They have been a source of comfort to countless faithful since they were first composed more than two thousand years ago.

After Talia's death, I came to understand one of its words, and consequently the psalm as a whole, in a new light. Take a moment to review it.

1 The Lord is my shepherd, I shall not want.

2 God makes me lie down in green pastures;

leads me beside the still waters.

3 Restoring my soul;

God leads me in paths of righteousness for the sake of his name.

4 Even though I walk

through the valley of the shadow of death

I fear no evil, for you are with me;

Your rod and your staff, they comfort me.

5 You prepare a table before me

in the presence of my enemies;

You anoint my head with oil; my cup runneth over.

6 Surely goodness and mercy will follow me all the days of my life,

and I will dwell in the house of the Lord forever.[6]

The first word of the final verse is customarily rendered in English as "Surely," giving us the familiar,

"Surely goodness and mercy will follow me all the days
of my life . . . "

However, the original Hebrew word is *akh*,[7] and it may not mean "surely" at all. According to Rabbinic interpretation, *akh* is a

6. Ps 23, *Holy Scriptures*; translation modified by the author.

7. אך

157

particle of speech indicating limitation or diminution.[8] Employing this definition, we can read the beginning of the verse as,

> "*A lesser sense of* goodness and mercy will follow me all the days of my life . . . "

If we have, in fact, walked through the valley of the shadow of death, we know full well the diminished sense of God's goodness and mercy that now accompanies us. Extending this understanding, we can render the conclusion of the verse, and the psalm, as, "*Nevertheless* I will dwell in the house of the Lord forever."

Having been under the cast of death's shadow, we are not the same people we were before. There is no sense pretending that we are. *Nevertheless,* walking along the paths that lead to righteousness remain the best paths upon which to walk.

8. *Jerusalem Talmud, Berachot* 9:14b.

## OVERCOMING FEAR

"Fear paralyzes hope and trust.
It cannot be defeated merely by intellect.
It needs to be overcome, in time, with courageous effort."[9]
—YANN MARTEL

The contemplation of death, whether our own or that of a loved one, is often accompanied by fear. We may fear we have wasted too much of our allotted time. We may fear we have not accomplished everything we set out to. We may fear that we will not recover. We may fear that our best efforts have been in vain. We may fear that we will lose more, and again.

It is true that such fear cannot be defeated by intellect. But some of it can be overcome with courageous effort, by refusing to give up. Doing so can help us appreciate that our losses, much less our fears, need not be the final word. Doing so can give us the courage to write a further and better chapter. Doing so can give us the hope that, in time, we will again know happiness and blessing. *Nevertheless.*

9. *Op. cit., Life of Pi,* Ch. 56.

## ON BEING BROKEN—
## FROM A CHRISTIAN, A MUSLIM AND A JEW

"The world breaks everyone, and afterward,
many are strong at the broken places."[10]
—ERNEST HEMINGWAY

"Keep your gaze on the bandaged place.
That's where the light enters you."[11]
—RUMI

"Ring the bells that still can ring. Forget your perfect offering.
There is a crack in everything. That's how the light gets in."[12]
—LEONARD COHEN

Hemingway says that we will all experience brokenness. Rumi says that the broken place is where new light enters. Cohen adds the reminder to "ring the bells that still can ring." In other words, to recognize that though we are diminished, new light will bring with it new healing, new opportunity, and new strength.

With such understanding we can go forward, *nevertheless.*

---

10  Hemingway, *Farewell to Arms*, 267.

11. Jalāl ad-Dīn Muhammad Balkhī, thirteenth-century Sufi mystic.

12. Cohen, *Anthem*, 1992.

## LIFE LESSONS

"I am not what happened to me. I am what I choose to become."
—CARL JUNG

In my younger years, I thought that life's goal was to find meaningful joy. I learned along the way that meaningful joy is not something we find, it is something we create.

I have also learned that it is essential to know how to overcome a broken heart. To do so requires the ability:

- to embrace life and its beauty once again.

- to hold fast to our better selves, especially during times of trial.

- to find ways to turn loss into blessing.

*In spite of everything* and *Nevertheless.*

# 17

# Conclusion

"There is strength in proving that it can be borne
Although it tear ..."[1]
—Emily Dickinson

## GRIEF IS PERSONAL

"Why me?" Most spiritual counselors have heard the question. It is at root, most often, an expression of anguish and grief.

Intellectually, we know that none of us is granted an exception to the laws of nature. Yet, we are still shocked when it happens to us.

Plainly speaking, why not you? You are mortal flesh and blood, living on the same planet as the rest of us. Chaos—random and otherwise—is never far away. It can happen to you as easily as it can happen to anyone.

The laws of the universe make no exceptions. We have no choice but to accept them.

1. Dickinson, *Poem #1133*, 1–2.

# CHARITY AND JUSTICE

"Establish the work of our hands that it may long endure."
—PSALM 90:17

The Book of Proverbs declares that "Charity saves from death." The phrase is repeated in the Talmud and other sacred texts.[2] It is frequently inscribed on Jewish collection boxes. Since giving charity does not prevent a person from dying, what is the verse trying to tell us? In the wake of Tali's death, I came to this understanding:

The Hebrew word for charity, *tzedakah*,[3] can also mean an "act of justice." The acts of justice done in Tali's name have saved both her and us from at least some measure of the terrible finality of her death. In tangible ways, she lives on.

Whatever God we may or may not believe in, whatever God does or does not exist, we retain the power to sanctify, or if you prefer, to elevate, our lives. We live beyond our years on earth when we give life, give charity, and extend the boundaries of justice.

That which has been done in Talia's name does not remotely offset the years of joy and accomplishment we would have celebrated had she lived a normal span of years. Neither does it remove our sorrow.

*Nevertheless,* charity allows us to make some sense and purpose of a tragedy that makes no sense by itself. Acts of justice are the blocks upon which we build life and legacy. However long we may live.

2. Proverbs 10:2; *Babylonian Talmud, Baba Batra* 10a.
3. צדקה

163

## WHAT IS LEFT

"Everything can be taken from us but one . . .
the ability to choose our attitude in a given set of circumstances."[4]
—VIKTOR FRANKL

Because ancient sages of every faith recognized that it was natural for people to question the existence of an all-just and all-powerful God, they filled their holy books with statements and stories of affirmation. These comprise the official version, if you will, of *Nevertheless*.

We may not accept all of their responses, but we have now put forth a set of our own.

Working to repair the world is a response. Pursuing justice is a response. Creating a worthy legacy is a response. Participating in the life of a sacred community is a response. Seeking to serve the God whose Law and Spirit point us higher is a response.

We can begin with this. We can go forward with this. We can sanctify life with this. We can bless one another with this.

*Nevertheless*.

4. Frankl, *Man's Search*, 104.

# FAITH CAN HELP,
# EVEN IF IT CANNOT (COMPLETELY) HEAL

When I was younger,
I believed the mystical teachings
could erase sorrow. The mystical teachings
do not erase sorrow.

They say, here is your life.
What will you do with it?[5]
—YEHOSHUA NOVEMBER, HASIDIC POET

Does faith have the power to heal us? If by heal, we mean remove our sorrow altogether, probably not. Even if we could somehow mystically merge into the Eternal One and lose all sense of pain and loss, we would return soon enough to our everyday duality—and its sadness.

But faith can still give us enough guidance and wisdom to pass the Tragedy Test.

Faith affirms that, in spite of a tragic ending, the life itself—no matter how brief—was neither meaningless nor futile.

Faith teaches that each of us leaves a legacy. It is transformed into blessing when it is translated into action.

Faith reminds us that sadness is inescapable. But it is possible to live with, and even overcome, some of it.

Faith holds that life is best lived when it is built on honorable purpose. If it has been, we have done all that it is possible to do.

Faith reminds us that a good name is the greatest crown.

All this can bring us—at least some—healing and peace.

5. November, *Two Worlds,* 14–15.

## TALIA'S LIFE—AND DEATH

"We can mend a torn garment
But it is still torn.
We can even dance in it.
But it is not the same."[6]

Numerous people have told us that Tali accomplished more during her short life than most people do over the course of many more years. That may be true. But as the Bible itself states, the reward for righteousness is length of days, not an early death.[7]

Who can escape the thought that after achieving what she did in twenty-six years, what she might have accomplished in thirty-six, forty-six, fifty-six or more?

On occasion, I allow myself to think that she is "up there," working with other exemplary beings, either on behalf of this world or another. I suppose it is possible. But it is ultimately unsatisfying.

Again, I've concluded that there was no metaphysical reason for her death. It was an accident, and it is not wrong to say so. Accidents happen, continually and often tragically, in our universe.

Earthquakes, hurricanes, volcanoes, and tsunamis bring devastation. Microbes and mutations cause dread diseases. Bombs and bullets cause collateral damage. Asteroids crash into planets. Quanta move at random. Motor vehicles hit joggers.

Accidents are an inescapable part of our world. They are, in essence, amoral. Our challenge is to emerge with a faith that accounts for them.

During this journey, I have concluded that living with faith in the God who is Law and Spirit is as good a way to live as any.

6. By the author, with gratitude for inspiration to Prof. Melila Hellner-Eshed.

7. Proverbs 3:1–2

Talia, too, dedicated herself to what was right and noble. It gave her life meaning. It brought blessing, goodness, and love to this world—and if you insist—to the next one as well.

Is it better to live a short life of meaning than a long one of emptiness? Though I suspect that yes is the correct answer, the pain is too great for me to say so. We continue on, *nevertheless.*

## TO LOVE AND TO MATTER

"And in the end, the love you take is equal to the love you make."[8]
—THE BEATLES

Talia Faith Agler has been influential in death because of the way she lived her life. She realized that service to others was a pillar upon which a meaningful life could be built. When any of us live by such lights, we too will be remembered and honored. And we will have mattered.

When we dedicate our lives to higher pursuits, we become a source of blessing. In what can seem like an indifferent universe, most of us want to know that we have loved and have been loved. We also want to know that we matter. The two are closely connected. As nothing else, love proves that we do matter.

It is almost always possible to increase the quantity of love and meaning in our lives. We can be a devoted member of a loving family or community. We can find additional ways to serve and teach others. We can work to preserve our planet. All of these enable us to become more than we would otherwise be. In the course of such activity, we can become partners with God.

§

We have seen why it is challenging to believe in the One God who is just. Much of the observable evidence does not support it, and much contradicts it. Still and all, serving the God of Law and Spirit, who asks justice and righteousness of us, remains a noble calling.

Serving this God will not answer every question. Nor will it guarantee pleasure or peace, though these may come. And it does not offer protection from hurt and sorrow.

It is, however, a path that provides us with limitless opportunity to create love and meaning. It is a path on which we can encounter blessing and healing. It is a path we can call Godly, and human beings can scarcely ask for more.

8. Lennon and McCartney, *The End*, 1969.

Our daughter Talia's life was short—but there is no question that it was filled with blessing. She touched the hearts, minds, and hands of many. She taught them to live with greater hope and to become more than they had been. In turn, their lives became blessings to others.

This was her passion, this was the God she served, this was her light, this was her life. She remains an inspiration and a force, even in death. She labored, she loved, she mattered. She always will.

# Afterword

"There is no meaning to life's absurdities—
other than the meaning we give them."

TALIA LIVES ON IN the memory of all who knew and loved her. The light in her eyes, the radiance of her smile, the depth of her thoughtfulness, companionship, and youthful wisdom will not be forgotten by anyone who knew her. She leaves a more public legacy as well.

## A. THE TALIA AGLER GIRLS SHELTER

The Talia Agler Girls Shelter (TAGS) is an arm of the Center for Domestic Training and Development in Nairobi, Kenya. Talia interned there as a college student and encouraged its growth as a professional. After her death, the Shelter was named in her honor. TAGS' mission is to reach, rescue, rehabilitate, and reintegrate trafficked and abused girls. It does so with astonishing success.

We are honored by the work being done in Tali's name and know that she would be proud of it as well. Go to cdtd.org for more information and to TaliFund.org to make a tax-deductible contribution. A portion of the proceeds from the sale of this book is being donated to The Tali Fund. Thank you.

## B. THE CAUSE OF ORGAN DONATION

From the time she received her first driver's license, Talia was a registered organ donor. Please consider becoming one, too. It is free and painless. It saves lives and families. Tali saved five lives by donating her heart, lung, kidney, pancreas, and liver. The stories of some of the lives and families she impacted can be found at the TaliFund.org website.

Is there any greater gift than the gift of life itself? Donors are needed. Even if you are subsequently rejected for medical reasons, the offer to be a donor makes a powerful statement to those around you. In the United States, go to organdonor.gov and register today.

## C. THE RELIGIOUS ACTION CENTER OF REFORM JUDAISM

After her death, Tali's friends and loved ones contributed to the Religious Action Center of Reform Judaism in Washington, DC. The funds provided scholarships to train college students to become social activists, both on campus and later in life. The RAC is devoted to keeping social justice at the forefront of the American agenda. Its values are very much a reflection of Tali's. See rac.org for further information.

Thank you for reading. May Talia's life be an inspiration to yours.

# Acknowledgments

I AM BEYOND GRATEFUL to the many friends, colleagues, and loved ones whose moral, spiritual, and literary support helped sustain me along this journey. It is simply not possible to name everyone and I apologize in advance for any omissions.

§

First, to my loving and beloved wife of forty-two years and life partner Mindy, Talia's more than devoted mom—simply put, there are no words. Thank you, ever and always, for everything.

To our son and daughter Jesse and Sarah, and their families and loved ones, we are grateful for you with every breath that we take. Nothing is more important to us than being your parents.

§

To my rabbinic colleagues who read the manuscript and offered insight and wisdom, I am much indebted.

The list begins with Rabbi Harold Kushner, author of *When Bad Things Happen to Good People,* who gave me the confidence to write on this complex topic in an accessible voice. Rabbis Jack Riemer, Marc Gellman, Stephen Wylen, and Yossi Liebowitz all provided general or detailed suggestions, encouragement, and critique.

Rabbis and scholars with whom I discussed the work in progress and have likely assisted more than they realize include Henry Balser, Steven Sager, Mark Mahler, Robert Wolkoff, Daniel

Alexander, Jeffrey K. Salkin, Lawrence A. Hoffman, and Melila Hellner-Eshed.

My lifelong friend Prof. Dr. Alan Fischler read an early version of the manuscript and offered caring and comprehensive analysis, along with encouragement. The comments and counsel of cousin Barbara Smalley, a many times published author, were similarly helpful.

In-depth editorial input, developmental, and linguistic critique came from Jami Bernard of Barncat Publishing in New York. Sam Vinicur in Florida was beyond generous and devoted in contributing his professional editorial counsel, literary expertise, and copy editing skills. The assistance of each of them was invaluable. My former student Steven Salpeter, now a literary agent, suggested pathways through the publishing world's many thickets.

Gratitude goes to Wipf and Stock Publishers of Eugene, Oregon, for accepting *The Tragedy Test* for publication and seeing it through to production. Special thanks also goes to Alan J. Harris, Esq., of Westchester, NY for his legal assistance and to Joel Agler, CPA, for his accounting counsel regarding the book and its charitable proceeds.

§

During the course of my life, I have been blessed with a number of great teachers who have helped shape the person I have (so far) become. I will identify just a few of them here. Sadly, none will be able to read this.

The most important were my parents, Gene and Sylvia Agler, who were worshipped by Tali—for an abundance of good reasons.

Rabbi Dr. Eugene B. Borowitz not only taught me how to wrestle with profound questions but also to present responses to them in a comprehensible fashion. I can only pray that this book is worthy of his surpassing standard.

Professor Dr. Irving Sarnoff's teachings on love and higher consciousness brought them, and so much more, into my life in extraordinary and abiding ways. He has been with me, in spirit, every day for nearly fifty years.

Gratitude, too, goes to Mr. Ronald A. Rotella, who nurtured his select class of would-be prodigies during our final two years of elementary school. He taught us, among many other things, to love learning and to be upright in all we do.

§

I am enormously indebted to the various rabbinic communities in which I am, or have been, active over the years. For enduring friendship and healing embrace, I thank members of the President's Conference of the Hebrew Union College–Jewish Institute of Religion; SEACCAR—the Southeastern Association of the Central Conference of American Rabbis; the National Rabbinic *Kallah* at Wildacres; and ONEG—the Organization for Networking, Education and Growth.

Key Largo's "Latitude 25" writers group and its leader Steve Gibbs, welcomed me as a newcomer and offered feedback on *The Tragedy Test* throughout the course of its gestation. Specifically, they helped me better understand how a broad and general audience might receive this book.

Mindy joins me in extending heartfelt thanks to the members of the Keys Jewish Community Center in Tavernier, Florida, who have provided us with a spiritual home in the years following Tali's death. It is a devoted community, one that has allowed us to share, teach, learn, laugh, and when need be, cry.

§

During the awful days of January 26-31, 2012, a large number of people helped keep us together in body, mind, and soul. The professionalism of the US Park Police, the staff of George Washington University Hospital, and the rabbis of Temple Sinai in Washington: Fred Reiner, Jonathan Roos, Mindy Portnoy, and Jessica Oleon Kirschner, were supportive beyond description. So too were Rabbi Dan Levin and the leadership of Temple Beth El in Boca Raton, who offered their sanctuary for the memorial service in Florida. No one should ever have to go through something like this, but anyone who does should only be cared for by people of this caliber. We will never forget.

Talia's extended family and friends, who dropped everything on that late January night and early morning to be at her hospital bedside, demonstrated what love and friendship are all about. Rachel, Stan, Peter, Jeff, Ellen, Gerard, Christine, Harlan, Raj, Kim, Jessica, we love you all. The staff and leadership of Chemonics, Inc. where Tali worked, were similarly beyond compassionate in their understanding and caring.

To each and every one of the more than 1500 people who offered comfort through their attendance at either or both of the services in Tali's memory, the family thanks you. Likewise to the hundreds who filled our home during the days of *shivah*. Your presence meant everything to us.

§

We are beholden to Ambassador Rabbi David Saperstein, Director Emeritus of the Religious Action Center in Washington, DC for his lifelong leadership in the arena of social justice. It was our honor to designate a portion of the initial contributions made in Tali's memory to the RAC, whose values so cohered with hers.

We are in debt beyond measure to Ms. Edith Murogo, founder of the Centre for Domestic Training and Development in Nairobi, Kenya. Her willingness to accept Tali as an intern led, as Mindy has described it, to "a match made in heaven." The Talia Agler Girls Shelter and the girls who have been rescued, rehabilitated, and reintegrated into society through its work are enduring testaments to their shared spirit and vision.

Talia's legacy is perhaps nowhere more concrete than it is in the lives and families of Martha Lefebvre, who received Tali's donated heart, and Brandy Swann, who received her lung. Her organs saved their lives, as well as the lives of three other souls whose names are not known to us. Through it all, we were blessed to know that her heart continued to beat, her lung to breathe, and in ways seen and unseen, Talia Faith Agler lived, and lives.

# Bibliography

Camus, Albert. *The Myth of Sisyphus*. Translated by Justin O'Brien. London: Hamish Hamilton, 1955.

Cline, Austin. *Albert Einstein Quotes Denying Belief in a Personal God*. ThoughtCo, May 14, 2018, thoughtco.com/albert-einstein-quotes-on-a-personal-god-249856.

———. *How are Religion and Science Driven by Mystery?* ThoughtCo, Mar. 22, 2017, thoughtco.com/einstein-quotes-on-mystery-249860.

Elliott, Doug. *What About the Groundhog?* https://dougelliottstory.wordpress.com/2016/01/15/what-about-the-groundhog/

Fitzgerald, F. Scott. *The Crack-Up*. New York: Esquire, 1936.

Frankl, Viktor. *Man's Search for Meaning*. New York: Simon and Schuster, 1959.

Goldberg, Rabbi Efrem. *What Are You Doing to Heal the Divide?* (February 10, 2012) http://rabbisblog.brsonline.org/what-are-you-doing-to-heal-the-divide/

Goodman, Micha. *Sodotav Shel Moreh Nevuchim—The Secrets of the Guide for the Perplexed*. Or Yehuda, Israel: Kinneret, 2010

Gottschall, Jonathan. *The Storytelling Animal*. Boston: Houghton Mifflin Harcourt, 2012.

Hemingway, Ernest. *A Farewell to Arms*. New York: Charles Scribner's Sons, 1929.

Heschel, Abraham Joshua. *God in Search of Man*. New York: Farrar, Straus and Giroux, 1976.

Joas, Hans. *A Conversation with Robert Bellah*. The Hedgehog Review: Vol. 14, No. 2 (Summer 2012) http://iasc-culture.org/THR/THR_article_2012_Summer_Interview_Bellah.php

Kaplan, Mordecai M. *The Meaning of God in Modern Jewish Religion*. New York: Behrman House, 1937.

Kelly, Albert Victor. *Education and Democracy: Principles and Practices*. Los Angeles: Sage, 1995.

Longfellow, Henry Wadsworth. *A Psalm of Life*. New York: E.P. Dutton, 1892.

Maimonides, Moses. *Guide for the Perplexed*. Translated by Shlomo Pines. Chicago: University of Chicago Press, 1963.

Martel, Yann. *Life of Pi*. Knopf Canada, 2009.

Maugham, W. Somerset. *Of Human Bondage*. New York: Grosset & Dunlap, 1915.

November, Yehoshua. *Two Worlds Exist*. Asheville, NC: Orison, 2017.

Renton, Jennie. "Yann Martel Interview." http://textualities.net/index.php?s=Martel, 2005.

Schultz, Charles M. *And the Beagles and the Bunnies Shall Lie Down Together*. New York: Holt Rinehart and Winston, 1984.

Voltaire. *Candide*. New York: Boni and Liveright, 1918.

Made in the USA
Columbia, SC
04 February 2019